TOE-UP SOCKS

·········· FOR ··········

EVERY BODY

Adventurous Lace, Cables, and Colorwork from WENDY KNITS

Wendy D. Johnson

NEW YORK

CONTENTS

INTRODUCTION

I probably don't need to convince you that hand-knit socks are wonderful. Most knitters seem to intuitively grasp the possibilities inherent in these tiny garments—the sizing that is easily adjusted to fit the wearer perfectly, the softness of the yarn that is a joy to behold and to wear. In short, socks are fun to knit. Still, some socks are more fun than others, and I am, and always have been, a fan of toe-up socks. I love not having to graft a toe shut, and I love being able to knit until I run out of yarn.

For years I was content to knit "plain vanilla" toe-up socks: straight stockinette stitch with a ribbed cuff. But there came a time when I started to think of a plain sock as a blank canvas. My first experiences with sock design were thrilling for me. I have always loved a challenge, and figuring out how to place a pattern in the finite universe that is the circumference of a sock has become one of my favorite pastimes. I enjoy doodling designs, whether lace or cable or colorwork, on bits of graph paper and knitting them up to see if they actually make a sock. And, I further entertain myself by figuring out how to make different patterns work in a variety of sizes—feats of mathematical gymnastics that I've included for each pattern in this book.

A few years ago, I started making my toe-up sock patterns available for other people to use. Some I posted as free downloads on my website, and others were sold through a retail outlet. Knitters responded to my modest efforts with praise, criticism, questions, and ideas. Through interactive dialogue with many knitters and through my own experimentation, I have refined my sock-knitting ideas and techniques.

A year ago, I wrote *Socks from the Toe Up: Essential Techniques and Patterns from Wendy Knits*, a book that contains all the information a beginner would need to knit toe-up socks. But, my toe-up adventures by no means ended there. In the intervening time, I have challenged myself to step outside my sock-design comfort zone and expand my world of toe-up patterns. *Toe-Up Socks for Every Body* contains twenty-one of these adventurous forays into sock design. I've tried to include something for everyone: dainty lace, intricate cables, and vibrant colorwork; traditional motifs and free-form inspirations; socks for women, men, and children of all ages, sizes, shapes, and dispositions.

Of course, sock-knitting veterans will find patterns to challenge and inspire new feats of sock mastery, whether altering socks to be knit as knee-highs, adapting a pattern to incorporate their own cable or lace motifs, exploring "sneaky" argyles, or doffing berets to thigh-highs with a certain je ne sais quoi. But if you have knit only plain socks, or are new to sock knitting, don't fear these patterns. They may look intricate overall, but remember that even the most complex pattern is knit just one row at a time. You will find that with a bit of care and attention, creating sock masterpieces that will impress your family and friends is much easier than you thought—and can be a whole lot of fun.

Each chapter introduces and explains the techniques necessary for the socks in that chapter, whether lace, cables, or colorwork, and I've included my favorite tips and tricks to ease your transition from sock newbie to pro. A breakdown of the most basic sock-knitting techniques and step-by-step instructions for toes, heels, and bind-offs, along with definitions for all of the abbreviations used in the patterns, can be found in the Appendix (page 127) for quick reference and instruction.

This book has been a labor of love for me. I hope that you will feel the same way about the socks you knit from these patterns. *May they warm your heart as well as your toes.*

PART ONE

basic information for sock knitters

BASIC INFORMATION FOR SOCK KNITTERS

If you are anything like me, you'll want to skip this chapter to dive in and start knitting. However, if you are new to toe-up sock knitting or to sock knitting in general, read on. You sock-knitting veterans should take a look as well because this chapter contains general information about my patterns and useful tips that can help make your knitting a successful and fun experience.

A toe-up sock is knit, you guessed it, from the toe up. You use a special cast-on technique to start your sock and then knit the foot from toe to heel, turn the heel, and then work the leg and the cuff. If you have never knit this way, or if you just need a refresher, all of the technical information you'll need to start knitting toe-up socks is included as an appendix to this book. The Appendix (page 127) contains detailed instructions on using the three different circular knitting techniques, step-by-step instructions for four different cast-ons, a description of the three heel techniques used, and, finally, step-by-step instructions for two nicely stretchy bind-offs for your cuffs.

....

TOE-UP TOOLS

Are you ready to jump in with both feet? Apart from your desire and enthusiasm, what else do you need to start knitting your socks?

sock yarns   The most important thing you need to knit a sock is, of course, yarn! All of the patterns in this book are knit from fingering weight sock yarns. If you are already a sock knitter, you likely already have a stash of sock yarns in myriad colors and fibers. And although a specific yarn is suggested for each design, you may find yarns in your stash clamoring for attention that will work up beautifully in the designs you choose to knit.

In general, socks demand a yarn that is easy to care for and can stand up to wear. Soft superwash wool with a tight twist is a good place to start, and nylon/wool blends will likely be more durable than 100 percent wool yarns. When knitting with cotton, look for a Lycra blend, which will help the sock retain its shape. Of course, nonsock yarns can be knit up into beautiful socks as well, as long as they can be knit firmly at the gauge stated for the pattern. Specific guidelines for substituting yarns and colors of your choice appear in each chapter to encourage you to make these socks uniquely yours.

needles   As you probably know, there are many different types of knitting needles out there. Everyone seems to have an opinion about which type of needle is the best, and I'm no exception. With all these choices, how are knitters to decide which needles suit them best? As with so many aspects of knitting, it's all about what feels most natural.

First, consider your favorite method for knitting in the round. Some knitters prefer to knit on five double-pointed needles, arranging the stitches over four of the needles and using the fifth to knit the stitches from needle to needle. Others prefer to knit on two short circular needles (16"–24" [40.5cm–61cm] long), dividing the instep and sole/heel stitches between the two needles. Still other knitters prefer the Magic Loop technique, which gets the job done with just one long circular needle. No single technique is better suited than another for knitting toe-up socks, so choose the one that feels most comfortable to you. The only exception is for the cable sock patterns in this book. For these patterns you will need to use two short circular needles. (See the Appendix, page 127, for detailed instructions for each method.)

Moving beyond the double-pointed versus circular debate, the type of needle you use can make or break your knitting experience. As far as I'm concerned, the pointier the needle the better. Because the socks here are all knit with fingering weight yarn at an approximate gauge of 8 stitches to 1" (2.5cm), you have some small spaces to maneuver through when working the patterns. Blunt tips on your needles will make this a lot harder than it needs to be.

And then there are needle materials to consider. Which is better—metal, wood, or plastic needles? My answer is an authoritative "it depends." If you are going for speed, metal is your best bet. The stitches slide easily off a smooth metal surface. Wood or plastic needles have a little bit of "grab" that makes it ever so slightly harder to move the stitches along the needle. If you are a newer knitter and fear having your stitches fly all over the place, choose wood or plastic needles with some resistance to help you put on the brakes as necessary. And, with colorwork, a needle with a bit of resistance will help you maintain even tension.

other tools Apart from needles, what else do you need to knit socks?

You might find stitch markers useful to mark out different portions of the design. If the pattern has a distinct center panel, you can place a marker at each side of it as a visual reminder to yourself. In addition, a row counter will help you keep track of where you are in your pattern. (And by counting rows, you can ensure that two socks in a pair will match exactly.) Other necessities include a tape measure or ruler, a tapestry needle for weaving in ends, and scissors. You also might want to keep a pad of paper or notebook and a pen in your knitting bag to jot down notes as you knit.

For cabled socks, many knitters use a cable needle, which temporarily holds the set of stitches to be cabled. It's fine to use this tool; however, I've also included instructions on page 56 for working a cable without a cable needle, because, ultimately, doing so will make intricately cabled sock patterns much easier and faster to knit. I have knit

every cabled pattern in this book without a cable needle (and you can too).

Another optional tool is a set of sock blockers, used to shape socks after washing. They are particularly useful for colorwork socks, as colorwork almost always needs to be blocked after knitting to smooth out the inevitable lumps and bumps. I don't consider blockers a necessity for noncolorwork socks, since the socks block out nicely when you put them on a human foot. But if you are giving a pair of hand-knit socks as a gift, blocking them first will make them look particularly lovely.

KNIT TO FIT

In most cases, I've written the patterns in a wide range of sizes to accommodate as many different feet as possible. Once you start knitting socks for a variety of people, you'll notice that there are a lot of different types of feet out there. For the most accurate fit when knitting socks, it's best to use the circumference of the foot as your guide. Therefore, you'll note that my patterns are all sized by sock circumference, and while I have noted a foot length in the size measurements, this is simply a guideline for an "average"-sized foot. When you work a pattern, you will knit the foot of the sock to the length you need.

To pick a size, measure around the recipient's foot and select the size that most closely matches it. You always want negative ease: The circumference of the sock should be slightly (10 percent or so) smaller than the circumference of the foot. This will ensure a nice snug fit without bagging.

What if you have a foot that doesn't match one of the pattern sizes offered? Look at the pattern chart, and see whether you can add or subtract part or all of a pattern repeat, or add or delete plain stitches on either side of a pattern repeat.

If the pattern does not lend itself to adjustments of this type, you can knit the top of the foot in one size and the bottom of the foot in another size. For example, let's say you want a sock with an 8½" (21.5cm) circumference but the pattern is written for either an 8" or 9" (20.5cm or 23cm) circumference. On your first round after completing the toe, increase 4 stitches across the bottom of the foot. This will bump the size of the bottom of the foot up to the 9" size while keeping the top of the foot at the 8" size, resulting in an 8½" sock. You may need to adjust the pattern further after you turn the heel, of course, depending on the size of the sock recipient's leg. You can decrease stitches above the heel to take it back down to the 8" (20.5cm) size, keep it at the 8½" (21.5cm) size, or add some stitches at either side to make it a bit bigger.

The important point to remember here is that a sock pattern is not set in stone. You are allowed—nay, encouraged—to make changes to it. If you are knitting for a foot or leg that does not fit nicely into one of the sizes offered, you can add and subtract stitches here and there to achieve a perfect fit.

Now, let's get back to the length of the foot. In all of the patterns, you are directed to knit the foot of your sock until it is a specific number of inches (or centimeters) less than the desired length of the sock before you start the gusset and heel. This will vary from pattern to pattern depending on the heel that is used. The number of inches or centimeters that you need to allow for the gusset and heel is noted in each pattern. Again, you want the length of the sock foot to be slightly less than the actual length of the foot to ensure a good fit. The best way to achieve a good fit is, of course, to measure the length of the foot for which the sock is being knit and then knit the foot length to about 10 percent less than that number. However, measuring the recipient's foot is not always possible if you are making socks for someone other than yourself, your immediate family, or your circle of friends, or if you want to give the socks as a surprise gift.

If you know the recipient's shoe size, you can get a rough idea of foot length. Many charts are available online (typically at websites that sell shoes) that convert shoe size into foot length in inches or centimeters. A word of caution, though: In my experience, a wide range of foot lengths are reported for a single shoe size among the various charts. It is a good idea to refer to a few different sites with this sort of information and average the results.

PATTERN ESSENTIALS

All of the patterns in this book are written with the stitches divided into two groups: the "top of the foot" (which becomes the front of the leg) stitches and the "bottom of the foot" (which becomes the heel and back of the foot) stitches. The two groups are referred to in the instructions as "needle 1" and "needle 2." However, this does not limit you to using two circular needles. You can split each of these two groups of stitches over two double-pointed needles, or you can put the two groups on each end of a long circular needle if you are a Magic Looper.

The only restriction when choosing among needle techniques occurs when knitting the cable sock patterns. In these patterns, you are directed to use a smaller-sized needle for the sole stitches (discussed in more detail on page 57). Unless you are an advanced knitter and able to consciously tighten your tension as you knit the sole and heel, you will not be able to use one long circular to knit at two different gauges. Instead, you must use either two circular or five double-pointed needles.

knitting from charts In addition to the written instruction, all of the patterns include a visual guide (or guides)—a chart. I love knitting from charts because I can quickly see the overall design and how the stitches of each row stack up. If you are new to charts, you need not fear them or feel that you have to translate them into written instructions before knitting. Think of a chart as a map for your pattern. It is simply a representation of a knitted pattern made up of symbols placed on a grid.

Here's a quick course on how to read a chart:
Charts for knitting are read from right to left and from bottom to top, just the opposite of reading text. Each square in the chart represents 1 stitch, and the symbol in that square tells you how to work that stitch. An accompanying key explains what each symbol means. Because you are knitting in the round for socks, you are always on a right-side row except when you are working the heel, at which point you are not using the chart. Therefore, each chart row is knit from right to left.

The good news is that socks are stretchy and are usually happy to conform to the foot they are put on, so chances are that even if the socks you knit are not a perfect fit, if you follow a foot-sizing chart and use your own powers of observation, you'll end up with a sock that fits pretty well.

a word about gauge Always check your gauge! Because a sock is a fitted garment, knitting to gauge is crucial. If you have a pattern that is supposed to be knit to a gauge of 8 stitches to 1" (2.5cm), for example, and you knit it at a gauge of 7½ stitches to 1" (2.5cm), a sock that is 66 stitches in circumference that is supposed to measure 8¼" (21cm) around will end up measuring almost 9" (23cm) around. This will make a big difference in the fit of the sock.

In the sample chart shown below, there are 13 stitches and 8 rows.

Row 1 of the sample chart is worked, right to left, as follows: K1, yo, ssk, k3, p1, k3, k2tog, yo, k1.
Row 2 is worked, again right to left, as follows: K13.
Row 3 is worked: K2, yo, ssk, k2, p1, k2, k2tog, yo, k2.
And so on from there.

The 13 stitches and 8 rows of the chart depict one "repeat" of the design. The pattern will tell you how many repeats across you will work. For example, if you wanted a total of 39 stitches, you would work the 13 stitches 3 times. And when you'd worked all 8 rows of the repeat, you would start over at row 1.

pattern difficulty   My intent for this book was to design sock patterns that were interesting and challenging, so some patterns will require greater concentration and skill than others. In each of the three pattern chapters in this book, you'll find a chart that explains the difficulty of each of the patterns in that chapter and any special stitches that are needed to knit each one. If you are unsure of your skill level, I suggest you start with one of the easier patterns and then move on to the more challenging ones. Advanced beginners or intermediate knitters who are familiar with knitting in the round and can follow instructions for the special stitches will be well equipped for most of the patterns in this book. Of course, I have also included a few patterns in each chapter to challenge experienced sock knitters. However, even these more challenging patterns are within the reach of a confident knitter who relishes learning something new.

key

	K
•	P
o	YO
/	K2TOG
\	SSK

sample chart

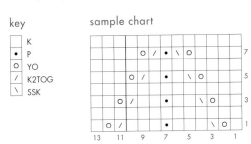

TIPS FOR READING CHARTS

If I am knitting from a small, easy chart like the sample on this page, I can usually memorize it. But if I am working from a large chart—for example, the Wrought Iron chart (page 77), which is 14 stitches across and 38 rows high—I will need some help. I use a metal project board and magnetic strips to keep my place in the pattern. By moving the magnetic strip up as I complete each row, I always know exactly where I am.

You can achieve a similar result by placing a sticky note on your pattern and moving it up as you work each row.

If I have a chart that has pattern stitches in "clumps" with several plain knit stitches between each clump, I will sometimes write the number of knit stitches in between each "pattern clump" on the chart. That way I don't have to count the plain stitches on the chart.

NEXT STEPS: DESIGNING YOUR OWN TOE-UP SOCKS

After you become adept at knitting socks to fit, at transforming socks to kneesocks to thigh-highs, and even at making changes to pattern motifs to suit your personal taste, you might find your needles begging for a new challenge. The truth is, if you can alter a pattern to custom fit it to a foot, you are well on your way to creating your own sock designs. Here are my top five tips for designing socks yourself. With a bit of persistence and some trial and error, you will be whipping out original sock designs before you know it!

1. Always have a sketchpad with you.

People often ask me how I come up with my pattern motifs. And, for me, each sock is different. Sometimes a particular yarn will speak to me; sometimes it's a flower, sometimes it's an architectural element—and sometimes an idea emerges full grown from my brain. Regardless of how far along an idea may be, the first thing to do is grab some graph paper and a pencil and start sketching!

2. Put comfort first.

With sketch in hand, analyze your pattern for wearability. Ask yourself how the stitches will lie against the foot. For example, will they create ridges and bumps that will be uncomfortable against a shoe? Generally speaking, you always want the sole of the foot to be worked in stockinette stitch so that the sock will be comfortable to wear. After you complete the toe, you can place a pattern on the top of the foot, but remember that it should not be too "bumpy" because it will be pressed against the foot while being worn inside a shoe. (*Note:* Bobble stitches on a heel are not particularly wearer friendly!)

You can vary the number of stitches on your sock a bit to accommodate your motif. But unless you are creating your own heel pattern, you'll need to increase up or decrease down to the proper number for a standard heel and then return to the proper number of stitches for your pattern after turning the heel.

3. Match your yarn to the sock.

As you design, you may find that you often build your socks from the yarn up, so to speak, but just as often you'll start with a pattern motif and select a yarn to fit. Remember that the more intricate the pattern, the plainer your yarn should be. Refer to the yarn guidelines I've given in each chapter for specific help in choosing yarns for lace, cable, and colorwork socks.

4. Knit a swatch.

You will always want to knit a swatch to test out your pattern. Remember that you are working your swatch flat, while the sock will be knit in the round. If you are doing a lace pattern with decreases and yarn overs on every row, you will need to do the purl equivalent of these maneuvers on the even-numbered rows (for the swatch only). Alternatively, you can knit a toe and then simply start your pattern on your sock, but be prepared to rip back if you find the pattern does not work for you. I usually work my sock swatches in this way because I like being able to knit my "swatch" in the round.

As you design, remember that fit is important. A sock should fit snugly. If you are designing using a very open lace, that will loosen up your fabric, and if you are creating a cable design, that of course will tighten your fabric.

5. Just knit it.

Of course, start with the toe. Use whichever toe-up cast-on method you like. I prefer a squarish toe, so I start with half the total number of stitches for the sock and increase every other row. You can start with fewer or more stitches, whatever you like.

As the sock takes shape on the needles, you'll need to decide on the heel you want to use. My favorite is the slip stitch heel because I like the extra bit of padding on the heel flap, but you can also do a short-row heel or some other heel. If you do a heel with a gusset (like the slip stitch heel), you need to start the gusset increases at the appropriate point as you knit the foot. You can do the gussets in plain stockinette or incorporate a pattern stitch into the gussets. Once you turn the heel, you can extend the design on the top of the foot around to the back or leave the back plain or work it in ribbing, and so forth. If you continue the pattern, you may need to increase or decrease a stitch at each side to make the pattern match.

Finally, you will work some sort of cuff on your sock, be it ribbing, a picot, or lace edge, or a folded-over hem. Many different edging stitches can be tried. You can extend elements of your design up into the ribbing. For example, if you have a cable on each side of your plain stockinette sock, work the cuff in ribbing but keep working those two side cables up into the ribbing.

One last word of advice: Remain flexible. Always remember that what looks good on paper does not necessarily work when knit up. As you knit, don't be afraid to make adjustments to your pattern. Very rarely do I knit a sock exactly as I sketched it out beforehand.

PART TWO

sock patterns

LACE SOCKS

Are you are intrigued by lace but find yourself intimidated by the almost invisible yarns and gigantic, intricate charts you need to knit an heirloom-quality shawl? Are you a lace addict who just can't get enough of the beautiful peek-a-boo patterns present in lacework? Socks to the rescue! Both the lace-phobic and lace-obsessed will find satisfaction in the patterns that follow.

the lace patterns at a glance

This chart lists all the patterns in this section, the special stitches used in each, and my assessment of their difficulty. Instructions for all necessary techniques are provided in the Lace Techniques section (page 20).

LEVEL	PATTERN	TECHNIQUE
✳	Rosebud Socks	single decreases, yarn overs
✳✳	Laurel Socks	single and double decreases, yarn overs
✳✳	Bouquet Socks	single decreases, yarn overs, 2-stitch cables
✳✳	Crocus Socks	single and double decreases, yarn overs
✳✳✳	Victory Socks	single decreases, yarn overs
✳✳✳	Belle Époque Thigh-Highs and Kneesocks	single and double decreases, yarn overs, leg shaping
✳✳✳	Dainty Anklets	single decreases, yarn overs, attached edging

For a lace sock, you will use the same techniques you would use to knit a much larger piece. Of course, in my opinion, the sock is a far more manageable project—I guarantee it can be completed much more quickly than, say, a 60" (152.5cm) square shawl. Further, socks are knit using a fingering weight yarn, which is far easier to knit with than a laceweight or cobweb-weight yarn.

For the record, there is a difference between "lace knitting" and "knitted lace." In "lace knitting," you are making holes only on every other row, whereas in "knitted lace" you are doing so on every row. The Rosebud Socks (page 22) are an example of lace knitting, as every even-numbered row is a plain row. The Laurel Socks (page 26) are knitted lace because each row has yarn overs and decreases. Knitted lace is allegedly more difficult because you are patterning on "wrong-side" rows. This may be true when you are knitting a shawl and are purling back on alternate rows. But when you are knitting socks in the round, you are knitting the right side on every row, which I find easier than working back on the wrong side. Just take care when decreasing that you do not catch a yarn over from the previous row, should the pattern require such a maneuver.

LACE TECHNIQUES

Have you never knitted lace before? Here's a crash course on the different types of increases and decreases you need to know to be able to knit the patterns in this section.

....

Increase—Yarn over (yo) A yarn over is made exactly the way it sounds: You pass the yarn over the needle between 2 stitches as if to knit to create an extra stitch. **(a)** On the next round, knit that yarn over. This creates a hole in the fabric. **(b)**

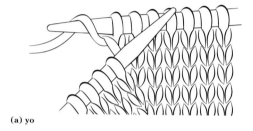

(a) yo

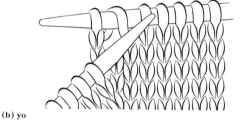

(b) yo

....

Decrease—Knit 2 stitches together (k2tog)

To k2tog, insert the right-hand needle into the first 2 stitches on the left-hand needle from front to back and wrap the yarn as if to knit. **(c)** Pull the loop through the 2 stitches, and allow these 2 stitches to slip off the left needle. You have decreased 1 stitch in a right-slanting decrease. **(d)**

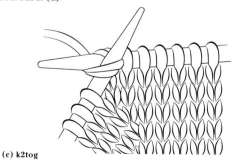

(c) k2tog

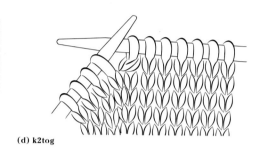

(d) k2tog

....

Decrease—Knit 3 stitches together (k3tog)

To k3tog, insert the right needle into the first 3 stitches on the left-hand needle from front to back and wrap the yarn as if to knit. **(e)** Pull the loop through the 3 stitches, and allow these 3 stitches to slip off the left needle. You have decreased 2 stitches in a right-slanting decrease. **(f)**

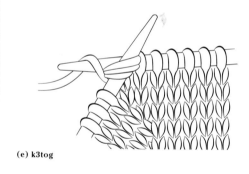

(e) k3tog

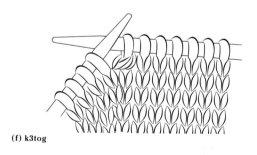

(f) k3tog

Decrease—Slip 1 stitch, knit 2 stitches together, pass slipped stitch over (sl1 k2tog, psso) Slip 1 stitch as if to knit from the left-hand needle to the right-hand needle, and then knit the next 2 stitches together. Now pass the slipped stitch over the stitch just worked, as shown. **(g)** You have decreased 2 stitches in a left-slanting decrease. **(h)**

Decrease—Slip, slip, knit (ssk)

Slip 1 stitch as if to knit from the left-hand needle to the right-hand needle, and then slip the next. Insert the left needle into the front loops of the slipped stitches and knit them together from this position, wrapping the yarn around the right needle and slipping the stitches off the left needle. **(i)** You have decreased 1 stitch in a left-slanting decrease. **(j)**

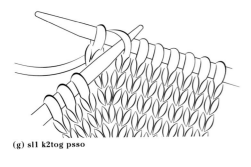

(g) sl1 k2tog psso

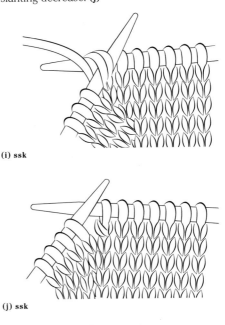

(i) ssk

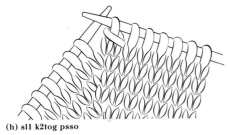

(h) sl1 k2tog psso

(j) ssk

YARNS FOR LACE SOCKS

A general rule when choosing yarn for lace is that the more complex your lace pattern, the smoother and less variegated you want your yarn to be. Textured yarns will obscure lace patterning, as will wildly colored, hand-painted yarns. For most of the lace patterns here, you can successfully use a yarn that is heathered or has slight variegations within the same color family. When in doubt, knit a swatch of the pattern to see how it works in the yarn you've chosen. For children's socks, you might want to use a yarn that has some nylon in it for added strength, as little ones can be harder on their socks than adults are.

rosebud socks

································

This sock incorporates an allover lace design that I think resembles flower buds, and I've used a yarn in a semisolid colorway that mimics the soft hues of roses. Although this pattern looks complex, it is surprisingly easy to knit, consisting of yarn overs, two different decreases, and some twisted stitches. Because the patterning is done only on the odd-numbered rows, you get a break on the even-numbered rows. The pattern is written in one size only, but the fabric is quite stretchy, so it will fit a variety of foot widths. Further, you can go up or down a needle size to adjust the fit.

SIZE M, 7"–8" (18cm–20.5cm) circumference, 9" (23cm) long foot, and 10" (25.5cm) tall leg measured from the bottom of the foot to the top of the cuff

GAUGE 8 stitches and 12 rows = 1" (2.5cm) in stockinette stitch

NEEDLES 2 US size 0 (2mm) circular needles (or 1 long circular needle), or size needed to obtain gauge

YARN 1 skein Dream in Color Smooshy Sock Yarn, 100% superfine Australian superwash merino, 4 oz (113.5g), 450 yd (411.5m), Lipstick Lava, (**1**) Superfine

TOE

Using a Turkish Cast-On, a Figure-Eight Cast-On, or Judy's Magic Cast-On, cast on a total of 30 stitches—15 stitches on each needle. Knit across the stitches on each needle once. On the next round, increase 4 stitches as follows:

Needle 1 K1, m1, knit until the last stitch, m1, k1.

Needle 2 K1, m1, knit until the last stitch, m1, k1.

Then knit a round without increasing.

Repeat these 2 rounds until you have a total of 66 stitches—33 stitches on each needle.

START THE LACE PATTERN

On needle 1, work the first row of the Rosebud lace chart over the next 33 stitches. Knit across needle 2. Continue in this manner, working as many repeats of the 24-row pattern as necessary until approximately 3" (7.5cm) shy of the total length of the foot.

CREATE THE GUSSET

Round 1 Work across needle 1 in the lace pattern. Needle 2 (sole stitches): K1, m1, knit across to the last stitch, m1, k1.

Round 2 Work across needle 1 in the lace pattern. Needle 2 (sole stitches): Knit all stitches.

Repeat rounds 1 and 2 until you have 55 stitches on needle 2. Work across needle 1 in the chart pattern.

TURN THE HEEL

You will now work back and forth on the stitches on needle 2 and will not knit the stitches on needle 1 while turning the heel. Turn the heel as follows:

Row 1 (RS) K37, kf&b, k1, w&t.
Row 2 P22, pf&b, p1, w&t.
Row 3 K20, kf&b, k1, w&t.
Row 4 P18, pf&b, p1, w&t.
Row 5 K16, kf&b, k1, w&t.
Row 6 P14, pf&b, p1, w&t.
Row 7 K12, kf&b, k1, w&t.
Row 8 P10, pf&b, p1, w&t.
Needle 2 now holds 63 stitches, having just completed a wrong-side row. On the right side, knit to the end of needle 2, knitting each wrap together with the stitch it wraps. Work across the instep stitches on needle 1 in the chart pattern.

HEEL FLAP

Work back and forth on the heel stitches on needle 2:
Row 1 (RS) K47 (knitting each wrap together with the stitch it wraps), ssk, turn.
Row 2 Sl1, p31, p2tog, turn.
Row 3 [Sl1, k1] 16 times, ssk, turn.
Repeat rows 2 and 3 until all side stitches have been worked; end having worked row 2. Turn your work and knit across, decreasing 2 stitches evenly on this row. Needle 2 now holds 31 stitches.

LEG

Begin working in the round again. Work the 33 stitches on needle 1 in the chart pattern as established earlier. Starting with the same row you worked on needle 1, work the lace chart over the 31 stitches on needle 2, *starting with the second stitch on the chart and ending having worked stitch 32.*
When your sock leg measures 9" (23cm) from the bottom of the heel, or 1" (2.5cm) shy of the desired leg length, work in k1 tbl, p1 ribbing for 1" (2.5cm). Bind off very loosely in rib.

ROSEBUD SOCKS

key

	K
ł	K TBL
•	P
O	YO
/	K2TOG
\	SSK

lace chart

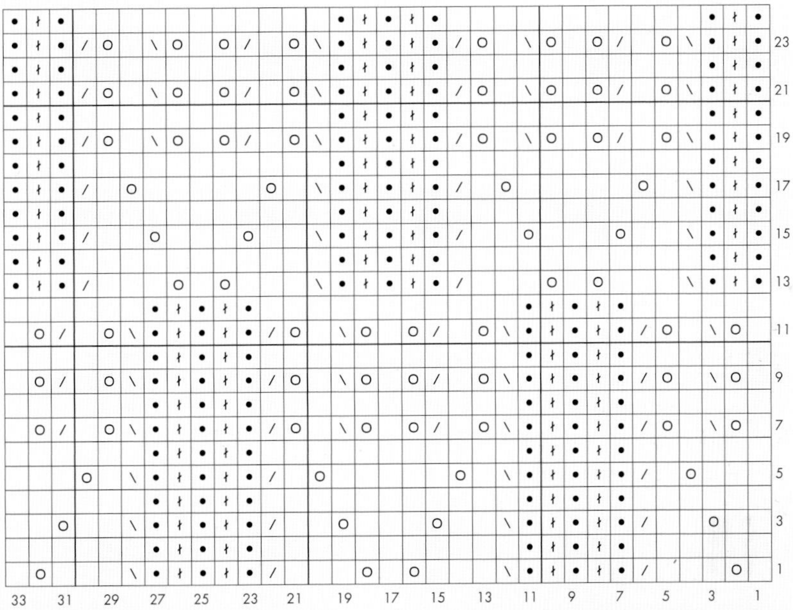

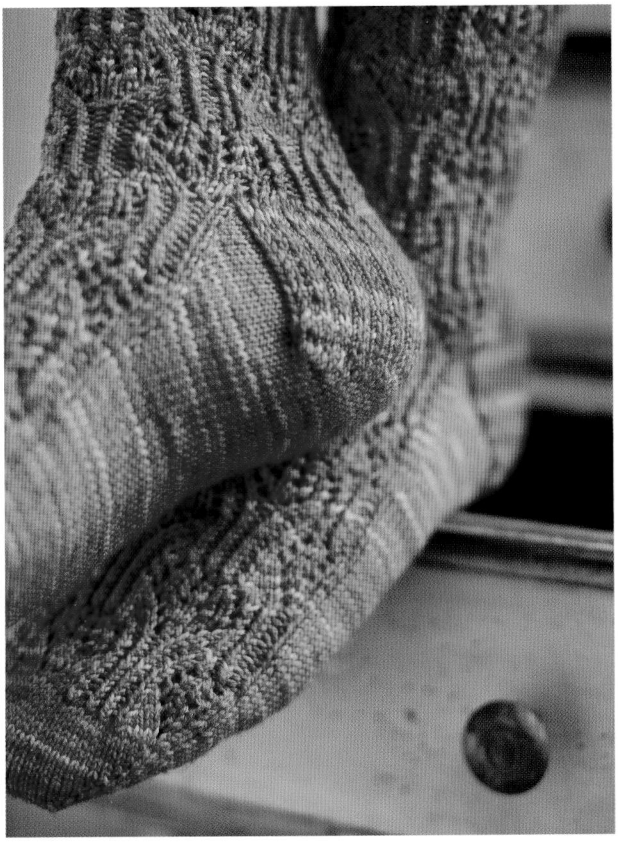

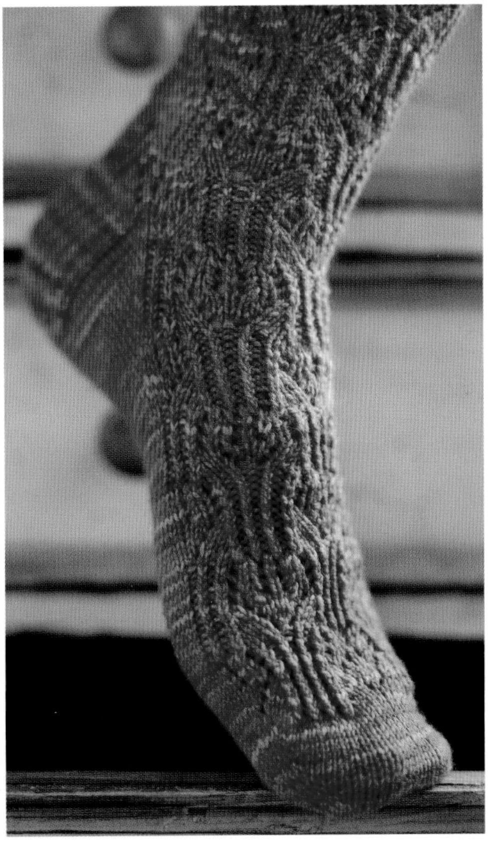

laurel socks

This design resembles a wreath of leaves and makes me think of the laurel wreaths once worn by victors in skirmishes, both athletic and martial. While it is an intricate-looking lace pattern with patterning on every row, none of the stitches used is particularly difficult to execute. I've written this pattern in a range of sizes that will fit older children as well as adults.

SIZE XS (S, M, L), 6 (7, 8, 9)" (15 [18, 20.5, 23]cm) circumference, 9" (23cm) long foot, and 9" (23cm) tall leg measured from the bottom of the foot to the top of the cuff

GAUGE 8 stitches and 12 rows = 1" (2.5cm) in stockinette stitch

NEEDLES 2 US size 0 (2mm) circular needles (or 1 long circular needle), or size needed to attain gauge

YARN 1 skein Dream in Color Smooshy Sock Yarn, 100% superfine Australian superwash merino, 4 oz (113.5g), 450 yd (411.5m), Go Go Grassy, **1** Superfine

TOE

Using a Turkish Cast-On, a Figure-Eight Cast-On, or Judy's Magic Cast-On, cast on a total of 22 (26, 30, 34) stitches—11 (13, 15, 17) stitches on each needle. Knit across the stitches on each needle once. On the next round, increase 4 stitches as follows:

Needle 1 K1, m1, knit until the last stitch, m1, k1.

Needle 2 K1, m1, knit until the last stitch, m1, k1.

Then knit a round without increasing.

Repeat these 2 rounds until you have a total of 50 (58, 66, 74) stitches—25 (29, 33, 37) stitches on each needle.

START THE LACE PATTERN

On needle 1, work the first row of the Laurel lace chart over the next 25 (29, 33, 37) stitches. Knit across needle 2.

Continue in this manner, working as many repeats of the 24-row pattern as necessary until approximately 3" (7.5cm) shy of the total length of the foot.

CREATE THE GUSSET

Round 1 Work across needle 1 in the lace pattern. Needle 2 (sole stitches): K1, m1, knit across to the last stitch, m1, k1.

Round 2 Work across needle 1 in the lace pattern. Needle 2 (sole stitches): Knit all stitches.

Repeat rounds 1 and 2 until you have 43 (49, 55, 61) stitches on needle 2. Work across needle 1 in the chart pattern.

TURN THE HEEL

You will now work back and forth on the stitches on needle 2 and will not knit the stitches on needle 1 while turning the heel. Turn the heel as follows:

Row 1 (RS) K29 (33, 37, 41), kf&b, k1, w&t.

Row 2 P18 (20, 22, 24), pf&b, p1, w&t.

Row 3 K16 (18, 20, 22), kf&b, k1, w&t.

Row 4 P14 (16, 18, 20), pf&b, p1, w&t.

Row 5 K12 (14, 16, 18), kf&b, k1, w&t.

Row 6 P10 (12, 14, 16), pf&b, p1, w&t.

Row 7 K8 (10, 12, 14), kf&b, k1, w&t.

Row 8 P6 (8, 10, 12), pf&b, p1, w&t. Needle 2 now holds 51 (57, 63, 69) stitches, having just completed a wrong-side row. On the right side, knit to the end of needle 2, knitting each wrap together with the stitch it wraps. Work across the instep stitches on needle 1 in the chart pattern.

HEEL FLAP

Work back and forth on the heel stitches on needle 2:

Row 1 (RS) K37 (42, 47, 52) (knitting each wrap together with the stitch it wraps), ssk, turn.

Row 2 Sl1, P23 (27, 31, 35), p2tog, turn.

Row 3 [Sl1, k1] 12 (14, 16, 18) times, ssk, turn.

Repeat rows 2 and 3 until all side stitches have been worked; end having worked row 2. Needle 2 now holds 25 (29, 33, 37) stitches.

LEG

For sizes XS, M, and L

Turn your work and knit across, decreasing 2 stitches evenly on this row. Needle 2 now holds 23 (31, 35) stitches.

Begin working in the round again. Work the stitches on needle 1 in the chart pattern as established earlier. Starting with the same row you worked on needle 1, work the lace chart over needle 2, *starting with the second stitch on the chart and ending having worked stitch 24 (32, 36).*

For size S

Turn your work and knit across, increasing 2 stitches evenly on this row. Needle 2 now holds 31 stitches.

Begin working in the round again. Work the stitches on needle 1 in the chart pattern as established earlier. On needle 2, p1; then, starting with the same row you worked on needle 1, work the lace chart over the next 29 stitches on needle 2, p1.

For all sizes

When your sock leg measures about 9" (23cm) from the bottom of the heel, or 1" (2.5cm) shy of the desired leg length, work in k1, p1 ribbing for 1" (2.5cm). Bind off very loosely in rib.

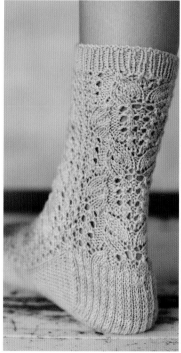

LAUREL SOCKS

key

	K
•	P
/	K2TOG
\	SSK
⋏	SL1 K2TOG, PSSO
O	YO

extra small lace chart

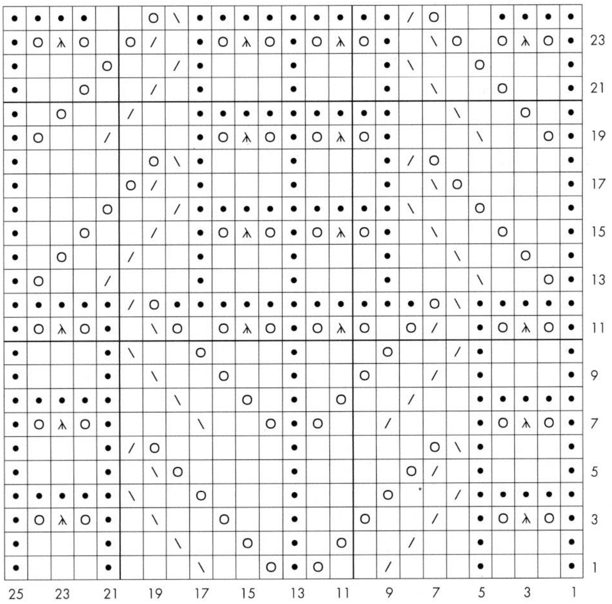

small lace chart

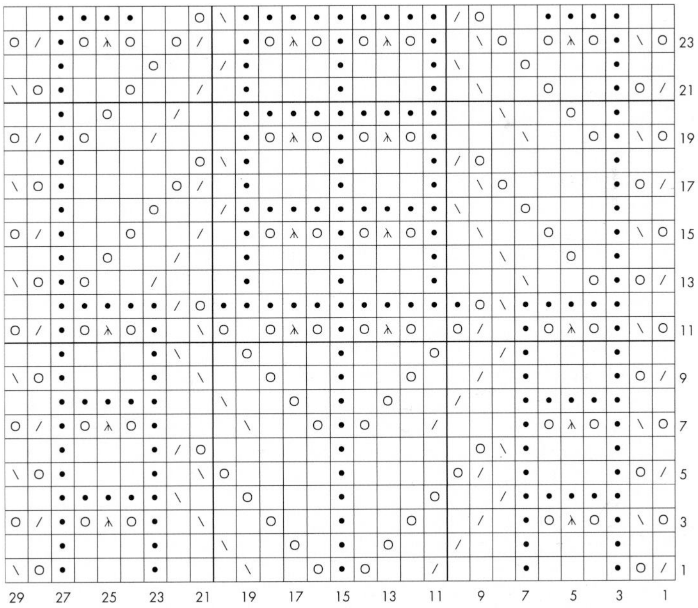

LAUREL SOCKS (CONT.)

key

	K
•	P
/	K2TOG
\	SSK
λ	SL1 K2TOG, PSSO
O	YO

medium lace chart

(rows numbered 1–23 odd at right; columns numbered 1–33 odd at bottom)

large lace chart

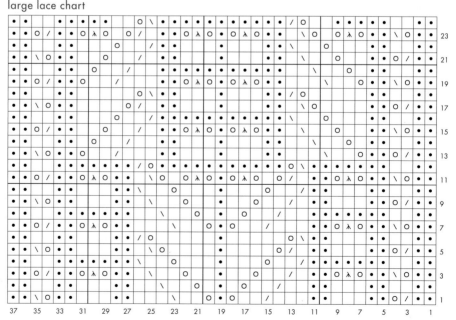

(rows numbered 1–23 odd at right; columns numbered 1–37 odd at bottom)

bouquet socks

bouquet socks

Have some cables with your lace! I love designs that incorporate both twists and holes. The leaves in the bouquets are formed by lace stitches and are complemented by simple cable twists in the stems. Because this design features a large pattern motif, you can use a slightly variegated yarn without obscuring the bouquets.

SIZE S (M, L), 7 (8, 9)" (18 [20.5, 23]cm) circumference, 9" (23cm) long foot, and 10" (25.5cm) tall leg measured from the bottom of the foot to the top of the cuff

GAUGE 8 stitches and 12 rows = 1" (2.5cm) in stockinette stitch

NEEDLES 2 US size 0 (2mm) circular needles (or 1 long circular needle), or size needed to attain gauge

YARN 1 skein Fleece Artist Basic Merino 2/6 Sock, 100% machine washable merino wool, 4 oz (113.5g), 370 yd (338.5m), Clementine, **①** Superfine

TOE

Using a Turkish Cast-On, a Figure-Eight Cast-On, or Judy's Magic Cast-On, cast on a total of 28 (32, 36) stitches—14 (16, 18) stitches on each needle. Knit across the stitches on each needle once. On the next round, increase 4 stitches as follows:

Needle 1 K1, m1, knit until the last stitch, m1, k1.

Needle 2 K1, m1, knit until the last stitch, m1, k1.

Then knit a round without increasing.

Repeat these 2 rounds until you have a total of 56 (64, 72) stitches—28 (32, 36) stitches on each needle.

START THE LACE PATTERN

On needle 1, work the first row of the Bouquet lace chart over the next 28 (32, 36) stitches. Knit across needle 2.

Continue in this manner, working as many repeats of the 28-row pattern as necessary until approximately 3" (7.5cm) shy of the total length of the foot.

CREATE THE GUSSET

Round 1 Work across needle 1 in the lace pattern. Needle 2 (sole stitches): K1, m1, knit across to the last stitch, m1, k1.

Round 2 Work across needle 1 in the lace pattern. Needle 2 (sole stitches): Knit all stitches.

Repeat rounds 1 and 2 until you have 48 (54, 60) stitches on needle 2. On the last round 2, increase 1 stitch in the center of the sole for a total of 49 (55, 61) stitches. Work across needle 1 in the chart pattern.

TURN THE HEEL

You will now work back and forth on the stitches on needle 2 and will not knit the stitches on needle 1 while turning the heel. Turn the heel as follows:

Row 1 (RS) K33 (37, 41), kf&b, k1, w&t.

Row 2 P20 (22, 24), pf&b, p1, w&t.

Row 3 K18 (20, 22), kf&b, k1, w&t.

Row 4 P16 (18, 20), pf&b, p1, w&t.

Row 5 K14 (16, 18), kf&b, k1, w&t.

Row 6 P12 (14, 16), pf&b, p1, w&t.

Row 7 K10 (12, 14), kf&b, k1, w&t.

Row 8 P8 (10, 12), pf&b, p1, w&t.
Needle 2 now holds 57 (63, 69) stitches, having just completed a wrong-side row. On the right side, knit to the end of needle 2, knitting each wrap together with the stitch it wraps. Work across the instep stitches on needle 1 in the chart pattern.

HEEL FLAP

Work back and forth on the heel stitches on needle 2:

Row 1 (RS) K42 (47, 52) (knitting each wrap together with the stitch it wraps), ssk, turn.

Row 2 Sl1, p27 (31, 35), p2tog, turn.

Row 3 [Sl1, k1] 14 (16, 18) times, ssk, turn.
Repeat rows 2 and 3 until all side stitches have been worked; end having worked row 2. Turn your work and knit 1 row, decreasing 1 stitch in the center of the row. The needle now holds 28 (32, 36) stitches.

LEG

Begin working in the round again. Work the stitches on needle 1 in the chart pattern as established earlier. Starting with the same row you worked on needle 1, work the chart over needle 2.

When your sock leg measures about 9" (23cm) from the bottom of the heel, or 1" (2.5cm) shy of the desired leg length, work in k2, p2 ribbing for 1" (2.5cm). Bind off very loosely in rib.

BOUQUET SOCKS

key

☐	K
•	P
o	YO
/	K2TOG
\	SSK
⤫	SL next stitch to cable needle, hold at back of work, K the next stitch, and then K the stitch from the cable needle.
⤫	SL next stitch to cable needle, hold at front of work, K the next stitch, and then K the stitch from the cable needle.

small lace chart

medium lace chart

27 25 23 21 19 17 15 13 11 9 7 5 3 1

31 29 27 25 23 21 19 17 15 13 11 9 7 5 3 1

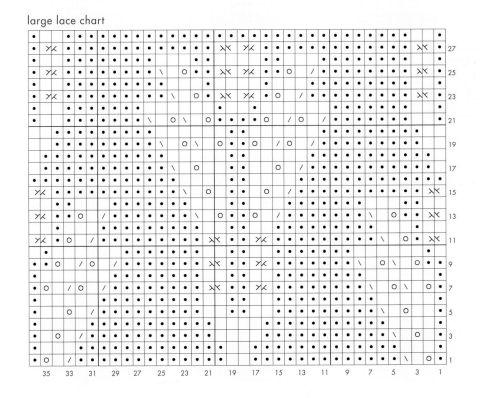

large lace chart

27 25 23 21 19 17 15 13 11 9 7 5 3 1

35 33 31 29 27 25 23 21 19 17 15 13 11 9 7 5 3 1

crocus socks

·······································

Although autumn is my favorite season, I can't help but feel a small thrill when I see the first crocus peeping out after a long dreary winter. This design is my salute to spring, and it features a large centered lace panel, flanked by small, mirror-image lace panels. If you knit these socks in the dead of winter, in a bright springlike color, I guarantee they will raise your spirits.

SIZE S (M, L), 7 (8, 9)" (18 [20.5, 23]cm) circumference, 9" (23cm) long foot, and 10" (25.5cm) tall leg measured from the bottom of the foot to the top of the cuff

GAUGE 8 stitches and 12 rows = 1" (2.5cm) in stockinette stitch

NEEDLES 2 US size 0 (2mm) circular needles (or 1 long circular needle), or size needed to attain gauge

YARN 2 skeins Louet Gems Fingering, 100% merino wool, 1¾ oz (50g), 185 yd (169m), Goldenrod, (**1**) Superfine

TOE

Using a Turkish Cast-On, a Figure-Eight Cast-On, or Judy's Magic Cast-On, cast on a total of 26 (30, 34) stitches—13 (15, 17) stitches on each needle. Knit across the stitches on each needle once. On the next round, increase 4 stitches as follows:

Needle 1 K1, m1, knit until the last stitch, m1, k1.

Needle 2 K1, m1, knit until the last stitch, m1, k1.

Then knit a round without increasing.

Repeat these 2 rounds until you have a total of 58 (66, 74) stitches—29 (33, 37) stitches on each needle.

START THE LACE PATTERN

On needle 1, work the first row of the Crocus lace chart over the next 29 (33, 37) stitches. Knit across needle 2.

Continue in this manner, working as many repeats of the 16-row pattern as necessary until approximately 3" (7.5cm) shy of the total length of the foot.

CREATE THE GUSSET

Round 1 Work across needle 1 in the lace pattern. Needle 2 (sole stitches): K1, m1, knit across to the last stitch, m1, k1.

Round 2 Work across needle 1 in the lace pattern. Needle 2 (sole stitches): Knit all stitches.

Repeat rounds 1 and 2 until you

have 49 (55, 61) stitches on needle 2. Work across needle 1 in the chart pattern.

TURN THE HEEL

You will now work back and forth on the stitches on needle 2 and will not knit the stitches on needle 1 while turning the heel. Turn the heel as follows:

Row 1 (RS) K33 (37, 41), kf&b, k1, w&t.

Row 2 P20 (22, 24), pf&b, p1, w&t.

Row 3 K18 (20, 22), kf&b, k1, w&t.

Row 4 P16 (18, 20), pf&b, p1, w&t.

Row 5 K14 (16, 18), kf&b, k1, w&t.

Row 6 P12 (14, 16), pf&b, p1, w&t.

Row 7 K10 (12, 14), kf&b, k1, w&t.

Row 8 P8 (10, 12), pf&b, p1, w&t.

Needle 2 now holds 57 (63, 69)

stitches, having just completed a wrong-side row. On the right side, knit to the end of needle 2, knitting each wrap together with the stitch it wraps. Work across the instep stitches on needle 1 in the chart pattern.

HEEL FLAP

Work back and forth on the heel stitches on needle 2:

Row 1 (RS) K42 (47, 52) (knitting each wrap together with the stitch it wraps), ssk, turn.

Row 2 Sl1, p27 (31, 35), p2tog, turn.
Row 3 [Sl1, k1] 14 (16, 18) times, ssk, turn.

Repeat rows 2 and 3 until all side stitches have been worked; end having worked row 2. Turn your work and knit across, decreasing 2 stitches evenly on this row. Needle 2 now holds 27 (31, 35) stitches.

LEG

Begin working in the round again. Work the stitches on needle 1 as established earlier. Starting with the same row you worked on needle 1, work the lace chart over needle 2, *starting with the second stitch on the chart and ending having worked stitch 28 (32, 36).*

When your sock leg measures about 9" (23cm) from the bottom of the heel, or 1" (2.5cm) shy of the desired leg length, work in k1, p1 ribbing for 1" (2.5cm). Bind off very loosely in rib.

CROCUS SOCKS

key

	K
•	P
/	K2TOG
\	SSK
⋏	SL1 K2TOG, PSSO
⋏	K3TOG
O	YO

small lace chart

29 27 25 23 21 19 17 15 13 11 9 7 5 3 1

medium lace chart

33 31 29 27 25 23 21 19 17 15 13 11 9 7 5 3 1

large lace chart

37 35 33 31 29 27 25 23 21 19 17 15 13 11 9 7 5 3 1

victory socks

These socks make "V"-shaped patterns and feature an intricate allover pattern that mixes lace stitches with twisted stitches with patterning on every row. The twisted stitches add a nice texture to the fabric and make it stretchy but sturdy. The pattern charts may look a little daunting because there is a lot going on, including twisted knit stitches, regular knits and purls, yarn overs, and decreases. Fortunately, the stunning result is well worth the effort. With careful attention to the pattern, you can award yourself a "V" for victory when you complete them!

SIZE XS (S, M, L), 6 (7, 8, 9)" (15 [18, 20.5, 23]cm) circumference, 9" (23cm) long foot, and 10" (25.5cm) tall leg measured from the bottom of the foot to the top of the cuff

GAUGE 8 stitches and 12 rows = 1" (2.5cm) in stockinette stitch

NEEDLES 2 US size 0 (2mm) circular needles (or 1 long circular needle), or size needed to attain gauge

YARN 1 skein Dream in Color Smooshy Sock Yarn, 100% superfine Australian superwash merino, 4 oz (113.5g), 450 yd (411.5m), Punky Fuchsia, **1** Superfine

TOE

Using a Turkish Cast-On, a Figure-Eight Cast-On, or Judy's Magic Cast-On, cast on a total of 22 (26, 30, 34) stitches—11 (13, 15, 17) stitches on each needle. Knit across the stitches on each needle once. On the next round, increase 4 stitches as follows:

Needle 1 K1, m1, knit until the last stitch, m1, k1.

Needle 2 K1, m1, knit until the last stitch, m1, k1.

Then knit a round without increasing.

Repeat these 2 rounds until you have a total of 50 (58, 66, 74) stitches—25 (29, 33, 37) stitches on each needle.

START THE LACE PATTERN

On needle 1, p1, work the first row of the Victory lace chart over the next 11 (13, 15, 17) stitches, p1, work the first row of the lace chart over the next 11 (13, 15, 17) stitches, p1. Knit across needle 2. Continue in this manner, working as many repeats of the 10- (12-, 14-, 16-) row pattern as necessary until approximately 3" (7.5cm) shy of the total length of the foot.

CREATE THE GUSSET

Round 1 Work across needle 1 in the lace pattern. Needle 2 (sole stitches): K1, m1, knit across to the last stitch, m1, k1.

Round 2 Work across needle 1 in the lace pattern. Needle 2 (sole stitches): Knit all stitches.

Repeat rounds 1 and 2 until you have 43 (49, 55, 61) stitches on needle 2. Work across needle 1 in the chart pattern.

TURN THE HEEL

You will now work back and forth on the stitches on needle 2 and will not knit the stitches on needle 1 while turning the heel. Turn the heel as follows:

Row 1 (RS) K29 (33, 37, 41), kf&b, k1, w&t.

Row 2 P18 (20, 22, 24), pf&b, p1, w&t.

Row 3 K16 (18, 20, 22), kf&b, k1, w&t.

Row 4 P14 (16, 18, 20), pf&b, p1, w&t.

Row 5 K12 (14, 16, 18), kf&b, k1, w&t.

Row 6 P10 (12, 14, 16), pf&b, p1, w&t.

Row 7 K8 (10, 12, 14), kf&b, k1, w&t.

Row 8 P6 (8, 10, 12), pf&b, p1, w&t. Needle 2 now holds 51 (57, 63, 69) stitches, having just completed a wrong-side row. On the right side, knit to the end of needle 2, knitting each wrap together with the stitch it wraps. Work across the instep stitches on needle 1 in the chart pattern as established.

HEEL FLAP

Work back and forth on the heel stitches on needle 2:

Row 1 (RS) K37 (42, 47, 52) (knitting each wrap together with the stitch it wraps), ssk, turn.

Row 2 Sl1, P23 (27, 31, 35), p2tog, turn.

Row 3 [Sl1, k1] 12 (14, 16, 18) times, ssk, turn.

Repeat rows 2 and 3 until all side stitches have been worked; end having worked row 2. Turn your work and knit across, decreasing 2 stitches evenly on this row. Needle 2 now holds 23 (27, 31, 35) stitches.

LEG

Begin working in the round again. Work the stitches on needle 1 as established earlier. Starting with the same row you worked on needle 1, work the lace chart pattern over needle 2 as follows: Work the chart over the next 11 (13, 15, 17) stitches, p1, work the Victory chart over the next 11 (13, 15, 17) stitches.

When your sock leg measures about 9" (23cm) from the bottom of the heel, or 1" (2.5cm) shy of the desired leg length, work in k1 tbl, p1 ribbing for 1" (2.5cm). Bind off very loosely in rib.

VICTORY SOCKS

key

☐	K
ǂ	K TBL
•	P
/	K2TOG
\	SSK
O	YO

extra small lace chart

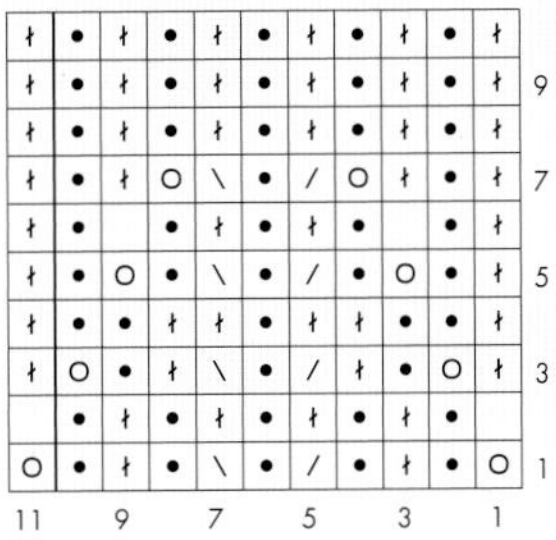

11 9 7 5 3 1

9
7
5
3
1

small lace chart

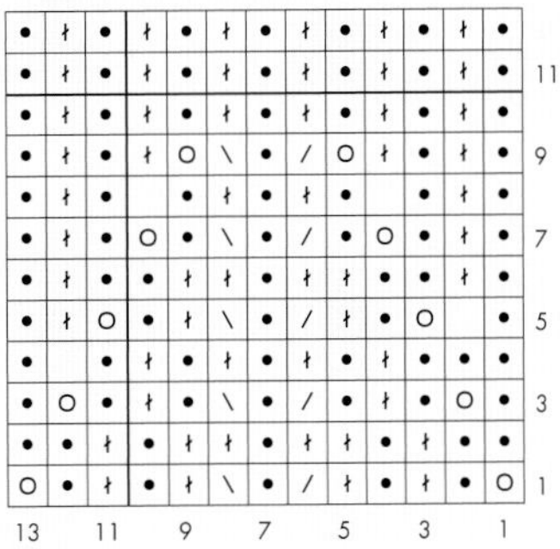

13 11 9 7 5 3 1

11
9
7
5
3
1

medium lace chart

15 13 11 9 7 5 3 1

13
11
9
7
5
3
1

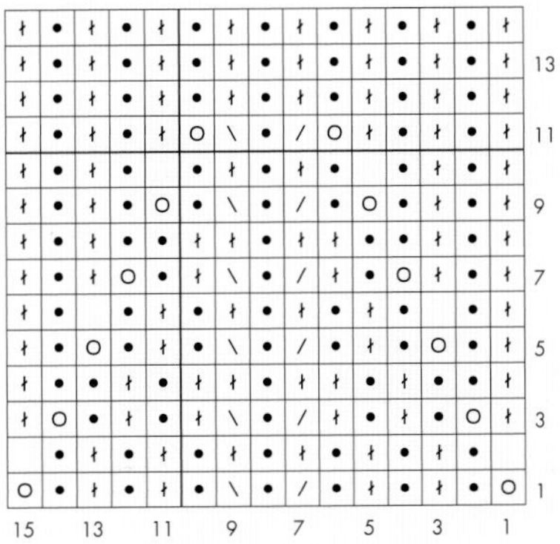

large lace chart

17 15 13 11 9 7 5 3 1

15
13
11
9
7
5
3
1

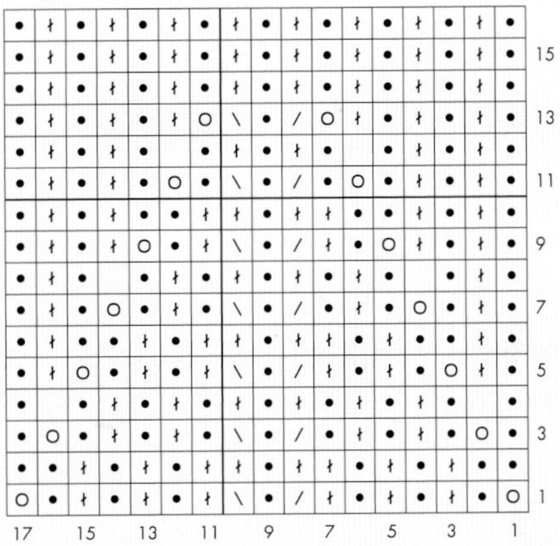

belle époque thigh-highs and kneesocks

....

These thigh-highs are reminiscent of stockings worn by dancers performing in the cabarets in the Paris of the Belle Époque. They are topped with an eyelet lace band, through which you can thread a pretty ribbon or an elastic cord, helping to keep the stockings firmly in place. For those who don't have the knitting time or the lifestyle for a pair of racy thigh-highs, I've included an option to knit them as kneesocks with a ribbed cuff. You could also adapt the lace cuff of the thigh-highs to the kneesocks, if desired.

Because of the nature of thigh-highs (and gravity), the yarn you choose is extremely important. Here, a blend of merino wool, nylon, and elastic is stretchy enough to accommodate a wide range of foot and leg sizes and elastic enough to hug the leg closely.

SIZE
Thigh-Highs S (M), 6¾ (7¾)" (17 [19.5] cm) circumference at foot, 9" (23cm) long foot, 16 (19)" (40.5 [48.5]cm) circumference at thigh, 27 (30)" (68.5 [76] cm) tall (unstretched)

Kneesocks S (M), 6¾ (7¾)" (17 [19.5]cm) circumference at foot, 9" (23cm) long foot, 10½ (11½)" (26.5 [29]cm) circumference just below the knee, 13 (14)" (33 [35.5] cm) tall (unstretched)

GAUGE 8¼ stitches and 14 rows = 1" (2.5cm) in stockinette stitch (unstretched)

NEEDLES 2 US size 0 (2mm) circular needles (or 1 long circular needle), or size needed to attain gauge

YARN
Thigh-Highs (Kneesocks) 8 (4) skeins Knit One, Crochet Too Soxx Appeal, 96% superwash merino wool, 3% nylon, 1% elastic, 1¾ oz (50g), 208 yd (190m), Berry, **1** Superfine

NOTE The knitted fabric for this design will stretch a lot due to the elasticity of the yarn used as well as the stretchiness of the lace design. Make sure you choose a size that is smaller than your actual leg measurements to allow the sock to stretch and hug the leg.

TOE

Using a Turkish Cast-On, a Figure-Eight Cast-On, or Judy's Magic Cast-On, cast on a total of 26 (30) stitches—13 (15) stitches on each needle. Knit across the stitches on each needle once. On the next round, increase 4 stitches as follows:

Needle 1 K1, m1, knit until the last stitch, m1, k1.

Needle 2 K1, m1, knit until the last stitch, m1, k1.

Then knit a round without increasing.

Repeat these 2 rounds until you have a total of 58 (66) stitches—29 (33) stitches on each needle.

START THE LACE PATTERN

On needle 1, work the first row of the 4-stitch Belle Époque lace chart 7 (8) times, k1. Knit across needle 2. Continue in this manner, working as many repeats of the 4-row pattern as necessary until approximately 3" (7.5cm) shy of the total length of the foot.

CREATE THE GUSSET

Round 1 Work across needle 1 in the lace pattern. Needle 2 (sole stitches): K1, m1, knit across to the last stitch, m1, k1.

Round 2 Work across needle 1 in the lace pattern. Needle 2 (sole stitches): Knit all stitches.

Repeat rounds 1 and 2 until you have 49 (55) stitches on needle 2. Work across needle 1 in pattern.

TURN THE HEEL

You will now work back and forth on the stitches on needle 2 and will not knit the stitches on needle 1 while turning the heel. Turn the heel as follows:

Row 1 (RS) K33 (37), kf&b, k1, w&t.
Row 2 P20 (22), pf&b, p1, w&t.
Row 3 K18 (20), kf&b, k1, w&t.
Row 4 P16 (18), pf&b, p1, w&t.
Row 5 K14 (16), kf&b, k1, w&t.
Row 6 P12 (14), pf&b, p1, w&t.
Row 7 K10 (12), kf&b, k1, w&t.
Row 8 P8 (10), pf&b, p1, w&t.

Needle 2 now holds 57 (63) stitches, having just completed a wrong-side row. On the right side, knit to the end of needle 2, knitting each wrap together with the stitch it wraps. Work across the instep stitches on needle 1 in the chart pattern.

HEEL FLAP

Work back and forth on the heel stitches on needle 2:

Row 1 (RS) K42 (47) (knitting each wrap together with the stitch it wraps), ssk, turn.
Row 2 Sl1, p27 (31), p2tog, turn.
Row 3 [Sl1, k1] 14 (16) times, ssk, turn.

Repeat rows 2 and 3 until all side stitches have been worked; end having worked row 2. Turn your work and knit across, decreasing 2 stitches evenly on this row. Needle 2 now holds 27 (31) stitches.

LEG

Begin working in the round again. Work the stitches on needle 1 in the chart pattern as established earlier. Starting with the same row you worked on needle 1, work the lace chart over needle 2, *starting with the second stitch on the chart* work stitches 2–4, and then work the 4-stitch lace pattern 6 (7) more times—27 (31) stitches total. Work on the pattern as set until you have completed a row 4 of the chart. Work the leg (instructions for thigh-highs are first; those for kneesocks are in brackets):

For size S

On needle 2, place a marker after stitch 11 and after stitch 16, so that the 5 center stitches on needle 2 have a marker on each side of them. Work 15 rounds in pattern. On the next round, increase 1 stitch on each side inside the markers by creating yarn overs, following the Belle Époque increase chart. Continue to increase 2 stitches in this manner every eighth round until you finish round 26 of the increase chart.

Move the markers so that they are on either side of the center 5 stitches again, and repeat the chart. Note that you will continue to work the 4 stitches of the lace chart and 1 knit stitch (total of 5 stitches) in the center as set as you knit the entire leg.

Continue to work the leg, making the increases every 8 rounds as set, until you have a total of 132 [88] stitches around.

Work without increasing until the sock measures 25" (63.5cm) [11" (28cm)] or until it measures 2" (5cm) less than the desired finished length (measured from the bottom of the heel).

For size M

On needle 2, place a marker before and after stitch 16, so that the center stitch on needle 2 has a marker on each side of it.

Work 3 rounds in pattern.

On the next round, increase 1 stitch on each side inside the markers by creating yarn overs, following the Belle Époque increase chart. Continue to increase 2 stitches in this manner every eighth round until you finish round 26 of the increase chart.

Move the markers so that they are on either side of the center stitch again, and repeat the chart. Continue to work the leg, making the increases every 8 rounds as set, and incorporating extra repeats of the lace chart pattern into the increases when you are able to do so, until you have a total of 156 [96] stitches around.

Work without increasing until the sock measures 28" (71cm) [12" (30.5cm)] or until it measures 2" (5cm) less than the desired finished length (measured from the bottom of the heel).

For thigh-highs (both sizes)

Work the top chart. Work the 12-stitch lace pattern 11 (13) times around the stocking. Work rounds 1–23; then work rounds 1–7 again. Bind off with a picot edge as follows:

Cast on 2 stitches using the cable method. Bind off 4 stitches, and slip the remaining stitch on the right needle back to the left needle as if to purl. Repeat until all stitches are cast off.

Cut a length of ribbon or elastic 30" (76cm) long, thread through the top eyelets, and tie in a bow.

Note To work a cable cast-on, insert the tip of the right-hand needle between the first 2 stitches on the left-hand needle. From this position, wrap the yarn around the right-hand needle as it to knit, and bring it through, between the 2 existing stitches. Transfer the newly created stitch onto the left-hand needle.

For kneesocks (both sizes)

Work in k1, p1 ribbing for 2" (5cm) and bind off loosely in rib.

BELLE ÉPOQUE THIGH-HIGHS AND KNEESOCKS

key

(blank)	K
•	P
o	YO
λ	SL1 K2TOG, PSSO
/	K2TOG
\	SSK
■	No stitch

lace chart

\	o		3
o	λ	o	1

3   1

small increase chart

Rows numbered (right side): 25, 23, 21, 19, 17, 15, 13, 11, 9, 7, 5, 3, 1
Columns (bottom): 13, 11, 9, 7, 5, 3, 1

medium increase chart

Rows numbered (right side): 25, 23, 21, 19, 17, 15, 13, 11, 9, 7, 5, 3, 1
Columns (bottom): 9, 7, 5, 3, 1

top chart

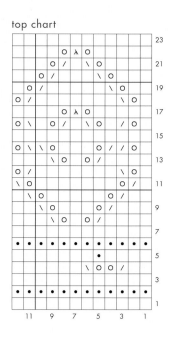

Rows numbered (right side): 23, 21, 19, 17, 15, 13, 11, 9, 7, 5, 3, 1
Columns (bottom): 11, 9, 7, 5, 3, 1

MAKING ALTERATIONS

You can alter the length of the leg of both the thigh-highs and the kneesocks by changing the rate of increases. For example, if you want your socks shorter in total length, you could increase every 7 rounds instead of every 8 rounds as directed, so that you reach the proper circumference sooner in your knitting and can make the sock shorter. Conversely, to make them taller, increase every 9 rounds instead of every 8 rounds. Remember that the row gauge is 14 rows to 1" (2.5cm), so increasing or decreasing the rate of increase by 1 row will make a difference of 1" in length after 14 increases.

You can also adjust the top circumference of this pattern to suit a more slender or more shapely thigh or calf. For the kneesocks, you can simply do fewer or more increases until you are satisfied with the fit. Because the cuff is knitted in a k1, p1 ribbing, you can add or subtract as many sets of increases as you need. For the thigh-highs, adjusting the top circumference is more complicated. The chart for the top cuff is based on a repeat of 12 stitches, so you must end up with a total number of stitches divisible by 12.

dainty anklets

....

Perfect for a tea party yet sturdy enough to withstand a day on the playground, these socks are as fitting for a demure young lady playing dress-up as for a rambunctious little girl scrambling through the neighborhood in overalls. The body of the sock is done in a simple eyelet stitch. There is a small amount of ribbing above the ankle, then a lace edging is knit sideways onto the live stitches, in the same manner you would knit an edging onto a shawl. My test knitter for this design, Marti Dolezal, suggested adding the loop and button to the cuff, and a very sweet addition it is!

SIZE Child's S (M, L), 5 (6, 7)" (12.5 [15, 18]cm) circumference, 6½" (16.5cm) long foot, and 3½" (9cm) tall leg (with folded cuff) measured from the bottom of the foot

GAUGE 8 stitches and 12 rows = 1" (2.5cm) in stockinette stitch

NEEDLES 2 US size 0 (2mm) circular needles (or 1 long circular needle), or size needed to attain gauge; 1 US size B/1 (2.25mm) crochet hook

NOTIONS 2 buttons, up to ½" (13mm) diameter

YARN 1 (1, 2) skein(s) Claudia Hand Painted Yarns Fingering, 100% merino wool, 1¾ oz (50g), 172 yd (157m), Baby Girl, **(1)** Superfine

TOE

Using a Turkish Cast-On, a Figure-Eight Cast-On, or Judy's Magic Cast-On, cast on a total of 20 (24, 28) stitches—10 (12, 14) stitches on each needle. Knit across the stitches on each needle once. On the next round, increase 4 stitches as follows:

Needle 1 K1, m1, knit until the last stitch, m1, k1.

Needle 2 K1, m1, knit until the last stitch, m1, k1.

Then knit a round without increasing.

Repeat these 2 rounds until you have a total of 40 (48, 56) stitches—20 (24, 28) stitches on each needle.

START THE LACE PATTERN

On needle 1, work the first row of the Dainty Anklets lace chart over the next 20 (24, 28) stitches. Knit across needle 2.

Continue in this manner, working as many repeats of the 4-row pattern as necessary until approximately 2 (2¼, 2½)" (5 [5.5, 6.5]cm) shy of the total length of the sock.

CREATE THE GUSSET

Round 1 Work across needle 1 in the lace pattern. Needle 2 (sole stitches): K1, m1, knit across to the last stitch, m1, k1.

Round 2 Work across needle 1 in the lace pattern. Needle 2: Knit all stitches.

Repeat rounds 1 and 2 until there are 32 (40, 48) stitches total on needle 2. Work across needle 1 in the lace chart pattern.

TURN THE HEEL

You will now work back and forth on the stitches on needle 2 and will not work the stitches on needle 1 while turning the heel. Turn the heel as follows:

Row 1 (RS) K19 (23, 27), ssk, k1, turn.

Row 2 Sl1, p7, p2tog, p1, turn.

Row 3 Sl1, k8, ssk, k1, turn.

Row 4 Sl1, p9, p2tog, p1, turn.

Row 5 Sl1, k10, ssk, k1, turn.

Row 6 Sl1, p11, p2tog, p1, turn.

Continue in this manner until all of the stitches are worked and you have 20 (24, 28) stitches on the needle.

LEG

Begin working in the round again. On the right side, knit to the end of needle 2. Work across the instep stitches in the lace chart pattern on needle 1. Starting with the same row you worked on needle 1, work the chart pattern over needle 2. Work in the chart pattern on the sock leg for 1 (1½, 2)" (2.5 [3.8, 5]cm).

Work 6 rounds of k1, p1 ribbing. Do not break the yarn.

WORK THE EDGING

With the working yarn, cast on 7 stitches on the end of the needle where you last worked a stitch. With the other end of the same needle, knit these 7 stitches. You will now have the 7 stitches just worked on your right-hand needle, and the sock stitches on your left-hand needle. Turn your work, and work row 1 of the Dainty Anklets edging chart back on those 7 stitches. Turn again, and work row 2 of the edging, knitting the last edging stitch together with 1 stitch of the sock

edge. Turn your work again, and work row 3 of the edging, slipping the first stitch. Note that you will bind off 2 stitches at the beginning of row 4. This will bring your total number of stitches back down to the number needed to work row 1 and will create a "point" in the lace edging.

Continue in this manner, working back and forth in rows on the edging, knitting the last edging stitch together with 1 stitch from the cuff on even-numbered rows. When you have knit up all of the sock cuff stitches, bind off the edging stitches.

FINISHING

Block the edging carefully by steam-pressing it while pulling the points out. Fold it down to create a cuff on the sock. With a crochet hook, crochet a small chain loop on one end of the edging; sew the button in the corresponding position on the other end of the edging.

DAINTY ANKLETS

key

	K
•	P
V	SL as to K
⊏	K st together with st from cuff
∕	K2TOG
\	SSK
o	YO
∩	Bind off

edging chart

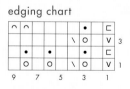

small lace chart

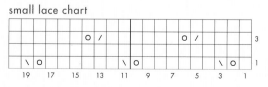

medium lace chart

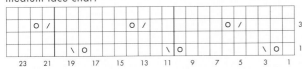

	O	/				O	/				O	/					3
			\	O				\	O				\	O		1
23	21	19	17	15	13	11	9	7	5	3	1

large lace chart

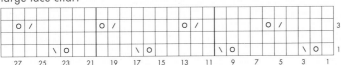

	O	/			O	/			O	/				O	/				3
			\	O			\	O			\	O				\	O	1
27	25	23	21	19	17	15	13	11	9	7	5	3	1

CABLE SOCKS

Cable knitting has an exalted position in
my pantheon of traditional knitting. It is
probably most well-known as a mainstay of
Aran style knitting, which takes its name
from the Aran Islands off the coast of
Ireland. Aran knitting combines different
complex textured and cable stitch patterns
to create a garment. The different stitches
used are symbolic of an island fisherman's
life, depicting, among other things, ropes and
woven nets. My first exposure to knitting
cables was when I knit a traditional Aran
fisherman sweater as a teenager. As soon as
I crossed my first cable, I was hooked. I have
knit many cable garments since that first
sweater, and I am always delighted to find
an intricate cable design I've not yet knit.

the cable patterns at a glance

This chart lists all of the patterns in this section, the special stitches used in each, and my assessment of their difficulty. Tips for speeding up your twists and turns by cabling without a cable needle, and for maintaining the proper tension for great-fitting cable socks, are provided in the Cable Techniques section (page 56).

LEVEL	PATTERN	TECHNIQUE
*	Heart to Heart Socks	2- and 3-stitch cables, lace stitches
**	Tiptoe Through the Tulips Socks	2-stitch cables
**	Manly Aran Socks	2-stitch cables
**	Wrought Iron Socks and Kneesocks	2-stitch cables, leg shaping (for kneesocks)
***	Diamonds and Cables Socks	2- and 3-stitch cables, lace stitches
***	Bob and Weave Socks	2-stitch cables on every round
***	Basket Case Socks	2-stitch cables on every round

Only recently did it occur to me to incorporate cables into my sock designs, and cable socks have quickly become favorites of mine. I am a traditionalist at heart, so some of the cable sock patterns here feature very traditional cable motifs, while others are my own modern interpretations. Creating cable sock designs requires some creative thinking. Cable knitting often appears very three-dimensional due to all of the twisting and moving of stitches. Many cable knit sweaters, for example, are highly textured and densely patterned. While this is wonderful for a garment meant to be worn while working on a cold, damp fishing boat, it is not appropriate for socks (unless you are knitting thick slipper socks for padding about the house). You will find that the sock patterns in this chapter have intricately patterned designs yet remain smooth and fine enough to wear comfortably in a shoe.

CABLE TECHNIQUES

Cable socks present their own set of rewards and challenges. Cables, by nature, pull knitted fabric in, so you have to take that into consideration when you are designing and knitting a cable sock. As far as I'm concerned, the more intricate a cable the better, but that can really slow you down when knitting socks. So I have some tricks I use when knitting cable socks to make the knitting faster and more fun. I'm happy to share my cabling secrets with you.

Cables Without a Cable Needle My favorite knitting trick is cabling without a cable needle. When I first learned to do this many years ago, my knitting speed increased dramatically. I encourage you to give it a try. For this tutorial, I use a 4-stitch left twist cable. This cable is traditionally worked as follows:

Slip 2 stitches onto a cable needle and leave at the front of the work, knit the next 2 stitches, and then knit 2 stitches from the cable needle.

To work this cable without a cable needle:
Insert the tip of the right needle through the second 2 stitches of the cable behind the work, and slip the left needle out of the 4 cable stitches. **(a)**

Slip the left needle back through the first 2 stitches in front of the work (the second 2 stitches remain on the right needle). **(b)**

With the first 2 stitches on the left needle, pull the needle back to the left to twist the cable. **(c)**

Insert the tip of the left needle through the 2 stitches on the right needle and take them off the right needle. All of your cable stitches, now crossed, are back on the left needle and you will now knit the 4 cable stitches. Your cable is complete. **(d)**

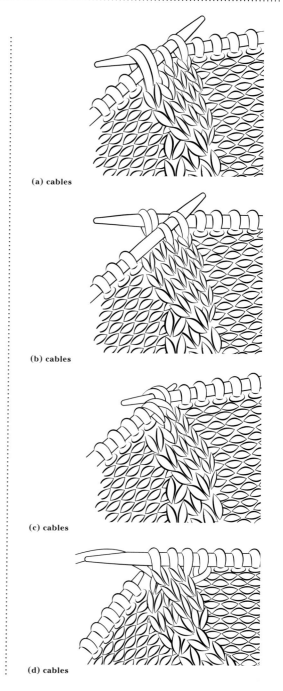

(a) cables

(b) cables

(c) cables

(d) cables

Tension for Cable Socks When you knit cabled socks, you must pay particular attention to tension. The cables should be loose enough for the sock to easily slip onto the foot and be comfortably worn while, at the same time, the "business" portions of the sock (the foot and the heel) must be knit firmly enough that they withstand wear. What to do?

My solution is to knit the sole of the sock and the heel with a smaller needle size than for the top of the foot and the leg. This is easiest to do if you use the two circular needle technique for knitting socks. That way, while you work the foot, your sole and heel stitches will be on the smaller needle, and the instep stitches will be on the larger needle. You can use this method with double-pointed needles as well, but you will need to remain vigilant to ensure that you don't mix up your needles. A good way to do this is to use a different brand or color for the needles of each size. This will not work, of course, if you want to knit using the Magic Loop technique. You could, however, use one of the other methods to knit the foot and use Magic Loop on the leg.

In all cases, you stop using the smaller needle after the heel is complete. The leg is knit entirely using the larger needles. The patterns direct you to go up one needle size for the cabled portions of the socks, but the more shapely the leg (or the more dense the cabling), the larger the needle size you should use. And if your sock recipient has large calves, you can go up another needle size partway up the leg to accommodate that shaping. If you are a particularly tight knitter, you might want to go up another needle size to account for this. Experiment to see what works best for you.

YARNS FOR CABLE SOCKS

Your best bet with cables is to stick with solid colors, or very slight heathers, as the cable work in most of these designs is very fine and intricate. Light and bright colors are a good idea, as they will make your cable work really "pop" for maximum effect. When knitting cables, I prefer to use a firm yarn with a tight twist. Because the yarn is being subjected to a lot of manipulation, you want a yarn that does not split easily. Using a yarn with a bit of nylon in it helps your socks to stand up to the extra manipulation needed to form cables. It also helps these textured socks wear well.

heart to heart socks

· ·

This is a relatively easy pattern that combines cables with a bit of lace. The heart-shaped motifs in the center panel are a combination of lace and cable twists. Small, mirror-image round cables flank each side of the center design. All of the stitches are pretty simple, and all patterning is done on odd-numbered rows only. The resulting sock looks far more complex to knit than it really is.

SIZE S (M, L), 7 (8, 9)" (18 [20.5, 23]cm) circumference, 9" (23cm) long foot, and 10" (25.5cm) tall leg measured from the bottom of the foot to the top of the cuff

GAUGE 8 stitches and 12 rows = 1" (2.5cm) in stockinette stitch

NEEDLES 2 US size 0 (2mm) circular needles, or size needed to attain gauge, and 2 US size 1 (2.5mm) circular needles; cable needle

YARN 1 skein Cherry Tree Hill Supersock Solids, 100% luxury merino fingering weight, 4 oz (113.5g), 420 yd (384m), Pink, ❶ Superfine

TOE

Using the smaller needles and a Turkish Cast-On, a Figure-Eight Cast-On, or Judy's Magic Cast-On, cast on a total of 26 (30, 34) stitches—13 (15, 17) stitches on each needle. Knit across the stitches on each needle once. On the next round, increase 4 stitches as follows:

Needle 1 K1, m1, knit until the last stitch, m1, k1.

Needle 2 K1, m1, knit until the last stitch, m1, k1.

Then knit a round without increasing.

Repeat these 2 rounds until you have a total of 58 (66, 74) stitches—29 (33, 37) stitches on each needle.

START THE LACE AND CABLE PATTERN

You will work the charts over needle 1 only (the instep stitches) and knit across needle 2 (the sole stitches). Knitting the stitches off needle 1 onto one of the larger circular needles, set up the pattern on needle 1 by working the first row of each chart as follows:

For size S

P1, work Heart to Heart chart A over the next 4 stitches, p1, work chart B over the next 17 stitches, p1, work chart C over the next 4 stitches, p1 (29 stitches total).

For size M

P1, work Heart to Heart chart A over the next 4 stitches, p1, k1 tbl, p1, work Heart to Heart chart B over the next 17 stitches, p1, k1 tbl, p1, work Heart to Heart chart C over the next 4 stitches, p1 (33 stitches total).

For size L

P1, work Heart to Heart chart A over the next 4 stitches, p1, k1 tbl, P3, work chart B over the next 17 stitches, P3, k1 tbl, p1, work chart C over the next 4 stitches, p1 (37 stitches total).

Knit across the stitches on needle 2 (keeping the stitches on the smaller circular needle).

Continue in this manner, working as many repeats of the 12-row chart B pattern and the 6-row charts A and C pattern as necessary until approximately 3" (7.5cm) shy of the total length of the foot.

CREATE THE GUSSET

Round 1 Work across needle 1 in pattern. Needle 2 (sole stitches): K1, m1, knit across to the last stitch, m1, k1.

Round 2 Work across needle 1 in pattern. Needle 2 (sole stitches): Knit all stitches.

Repeat rounds 1 and 2 until you have 49 (55, 61) stitches on needle 2. Work across needle 1 in the chart patterns.

TURN THE HEEL

You will now work back and forth on the stitches on needle 2 and will not knit the stitches on needle 1 while turning the heel. Turn the heel as follows:

Row 1 (RS) K33 (37, 41), kf&b, k1, w&t.
Row 2 P20 (22, 24), pf&b, p1, w&t.
Row 3 K18 (20, 22), kf&b, k1, w&t.
Row 4 P16 (18, 20), pf&b, p1, w&t.
Row 5 K14 (16, 18), kf&b, k1, w&t.
Row 6 P12 (14, 16), pf&b, p1, w&t.
Row 7 K10 (12, 14), kf&b, k1, w&t.
Row 8 P8 (10, 12), pf&b, p1, w&t.
Needle 2 now holds 57 (63, 69) stitches, having just completed a wrong-side row. On the right side, knit to the end of needle 2, knitting each wrap together with the stitch it wraps. Work across the instep stitches on needle 1 in the chart patterns.

HEEL FLAP

Work back and forth on the heel stitches on needle 2:

Row 1 (RS) K42 (47, 52) (knitting each wrap together with the stitch it wraps), ssk, turn.
Row 2 Sl1, p27 (31, 35), p2tog, turn.
Row 3 [Sl1, k1] 14 (16, 18) times, ssk, turn.
Repeat rows 2 and 3 until all side stitches have been worked; end

having worked row 2. Turn your work and knit across, increasing 2 stitches evenly on this row. Needle 2 now holds 31 (35, 39) stitches.

LEG

Work across needle 1 in the chart patterns.

Knitting the stitches off needle 2 onto the second of the larger circular needles and, making sure that you are starting on the same row of the charts as you are working on needle 1, work across the larger needle as follows: K1 tbl, work across the charts in the same manner as described for needle 1, k1 tbl.

You are now using both of the larger needles to knit the sock—you will not need the smaller needles again for this sock.

When your sock leg measures about 9" (23cm) from the bottom of the heel, or 1" (2.5cm) shy of the desired leg length, work in k1 tbl, p1 ribbing for 1" (2.5cm). Bind off very loosely in rib.

HEART TO HEART SOCKS

key

⸸	K TBL
•	P
o	YO
/	K2TOG
\	SSK
⸜⊤	SL next stitch to cable needle, hold at back of work, K TBL the next stitch, and then P the stitch from the cable needle.
⊤⸝	SL next stitch to cable needle, hold at front of work, P the next stitch, and then K TBL the stitch from the cable needle.
⸝⊤	SL next stitch to cable needle, hold at back of work, K TBL the next stitch, and then K TBL the stitch from the cable needle.
⊤⸝	SL next stitch to cable needle, hold at front of work, K TBL the next stitch, and then K TBL the stitch from the cable needle.
⊤ ⊤ ⸝	SL next 2 stitches to cable needle, hold at front of work, P the next stitch, and then K TBL the 2 stitches from the cable needle.
⸝ ⊤ ⊤	SL next stitch to cable needle, hold at back of work, K TBL the next 2 stitches, and then P the stitch from the cable needle.

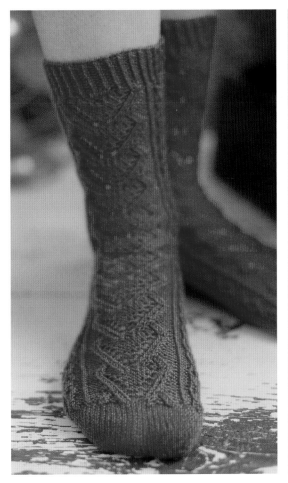
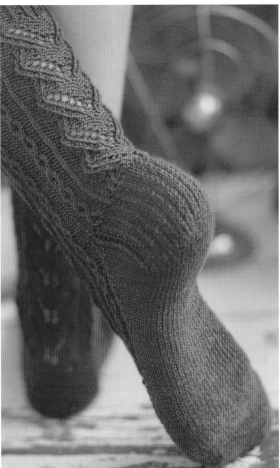

chart a

Row numbers: 5, 3, 1

Bottom: 3 1

chart b

Row numbers (right side): 11, 9, 7, 5, 3, 1

Column numbers (bottom): 17 15 13 11 9 7 5 3 1

chart c

Row numbers: 5, 3, 1

Bottom: 3 1

tiptoe through the tulips socks

....

Tulips are another of my favorite harbingers of spring. These fun socks have an overall design of small tulip cables that are easy to knit in twisted stitches, with patterning done on odd-numbered rows only. Don't be alarmed by the number of charts presented for this pattern. You will use different charts for the front and back of the leg because of the way the pattern motif is offset.

SIZE S (M, L), 7 (8, 9)" (18 [20.5, 23]cm) circumference, 9" (23cm) long foot, and 10" (25.5cm) tall leg measured from the bottom of the foot to the top of the cuff

NEEDLES 2 US size 0 (2mm) circular needles, or size needed to attain gauge, and 2 US size 1 (2.5mm) circular needles; cable needle

GAUGE 8 stitches and 12 rows = 1" (2.5cm) in stockinette stitch

YARN 2 skeins Louet Gems Fingering, 100% merino wool, 1¾ oz (50g), 185 yd (169m), Lilac, **1** Superfine

TOE

Using the smaller needles and a Turkish Cast-On, a Figure-Eight Cast-On, or Judy's Magic Cast-On, cast on a total of 28 (32, 36) stitches—14 (16, 18) stitches on each needle. Knit across the stitches on each needle once. On the next round, increase 4 stitches as follows:

Needle 1 K1, m1, knit until the last stitch, m1, k1.

Needle 2 K1, m1, knit until the last stitch, m1, k1.

Then knit a round without increasing.

Repeat these 2 rounds until you have a total of 56 (64, 72) stitches—28 (32, 36) stitches on each needle.

START THE CABLE PATTERN

You will work the chart over needle 1 only (the instep stitches) and knit across needle 2 (the sole stitches). Knitting the stitches off needle 1 onto one of the larger circular needles, work row 1 of Tulips chart A over the 28 (32, 36) stitches on needle 1. Knit across the stitches on needle 2 (keeping the stitches on the smaller circular needle). Continue in this manner, working as many repeats of the 20-row pattern

as necessary until approximately 3" (7.5cm) shy of the total length of the foot.

CREATE THE GUSSET

Round 1 Work across needle 1 in the cable pattern. Needle 2 (sole stitches): K1, m1, knit across to the last stitch, m1, k1.

Round 2 Work across needle 1 in the cable pattern. Needle 2 (sole stitches): Knit all stitches.

Repeat rounds 1 and 2 until you have 48 (54, 60) stitches on needle 2. On the last round 2, increase 1 stitch in the center of the sole for a total of 49 (55, 61) stitches. Work across needle 1 in the chart pattern.

TIPTOE THROUGH THE TULIPS SOCKS (CONT.)

key

ɫ	K TBL
•	P
⤸T	SL next stitch to cable needle, hold at back of work, K the next stitch TBL, and then P the stitch from the cable needle.
T⤵	SL next stitch to cable needle, hold at front of work, P the next stitch, and then K TBL the stitch from the cable needle.
⤸T	SL next stitch to cable needle, hold at back of work, K the next stitch TBL, and then K TBL the stitch from the cable needle.
T⤵	SL next stitch to cable needle, hold at front of work, K TBL the next stitch, and then K TBL the stitch from the cable needle.

medium chart a

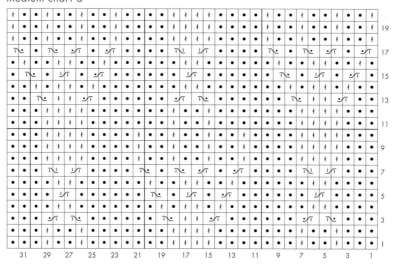

medium chart b

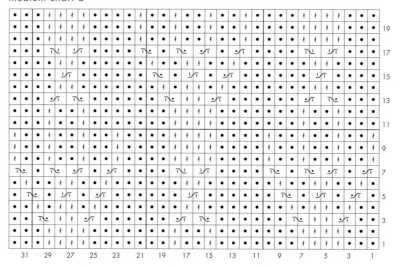

large chart a

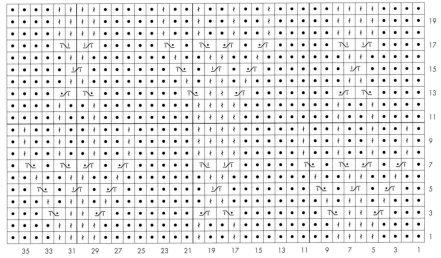

large chart b

manly aran socks

·······························

While many of the socks in this section are unisex, these socks are designed and sized specifically for men. I created this design to resemble an Aran fisherman knit sweater, with a large center motif flanked by smaller motifs on either side. The cables are clean and masculine without a hint of fussiness. The cable twists are done on odd-numbered rows only, so you get a break on every other row.

SIZE M (L), 9 (10)" (23 [25.5]cm) circumference, 10" (25.5cm) long foot, and 12½" (32cm) tall leg measured from the bottom of the foot to the top of the cuff

GAUGE 8 stitches and 12 rows = 1" (2.5cm) in stockinette stitch

NEEDLES 2 US size 0 (2mm) circular needles, or size needed to attain gauge, and 2 US size 1 (2.5mm) circular needles; cable needle

YARN 2 skeins Lorna's Laces Shepherd Sock, 80% superwash wool and 20% nylon, 2 oz (56.5g), 215 yd (196.5m), Denim, ❶ Superfine

TOE

Using the smaller needles and a Turkish Cast-On, a Figure-Eight Cast-On, or Judy's Magic Cast-On, cast on a total of 32 (40) stitches—16 (20) stitches on each needle. Knit across the stitches on each needle once. On the next round, increase 4 stitches as follows:

Needle 1 K1, m1, knit until the last stitch, m1, k1.

Needle 2 K1, m1, knit until the last stitch, m1, k1.

Then knit a round without increasing.

Repeat these 2 rounds until you have a total of 72 (80) stitches—36 (40) stitches on each needle.

START THE CABLE PATTERN

You will work the charts over needle 1 only (the instep stitches) and knit across needle 2 (the sole stitches). Knitting the stitches off needle 1 onto one of the larger circular needles, set up the pattern as follows:

P1 (2), work row 1 of Manly Aran chart A over the next 4 stitches, p1 (2), k1 tbl, p1, work row 1 of Manly Aran chart B over the next 20 stitches, p1, k1 tbl, p1 (2), work row 1 of Manly Aran chart A over the next 4 stitches, p1 (2).

Knit across the stitches on needle 2 (keeping the stitches on the smaller circular needle).

Continue in this manner, working as many repeats of the 8-row chart A and the 24-row chart B pattern as necessary until approximately 3" (7.5cm) shy of the total length of the foot.

CREATE THE GUSSET

Round 1 Work across needle 1 in the cable pattern. Needle 2 (sole stitches): K1, m1, knit across to the last stitch, m1, k1.

Round 2 Work across needle 1 in the cable pattern. Needle 2 (sole stitches): Knit all stitches.

Repeat rounds 1 and 2 until you have 60 (66) stitches on needle 2. On the last repeat of round 2, increase 1 stitch in the center of the needle so that you have 61 (67) stitches total on needle 2. Work across needle 1 in the chart patterns.

TURN THE HEEL

You will now work back and forth on the stitches on needle 2 and will not knit the stitches on needle 1 while turning the heel. Turn the heel as follows:

Row 1 (RS) K41 (45), kf&b, k1, w&t.
Row 2 P24 (26), pf&b, p1, w&t.
Row 3 K22 (24), kf&b, k1, w&t.
Row 4 P20 (22), pf&b, p1, w&t.
Row 5 K18 (20), kf&b, k1, w&t.
Row 6 P16 (18), pf&b, p1, w&t.
Row 7 K14 (16), kf&b, k1, w&t.
Row 8 P12 (14), pf&b, p1, w&t.
Needle 2 now holds 69 (75) stitches, having just completed a wrong-side row. On the right side, knit to the end of needle 2, knitting each wrap together with the stitch it wraps. Work across the instep stitches on needle 1 in the chart patterns.

HEEL FLAP

Work back and forth on the heel stitches on needle 2:

Row 1 (RS) K52 (57) (knitting each wrap together with the stitch it wraps), ssk, turn.
Row 2 Sl1, p35 (39), p2tog, turn.
Row 3 [Sl1, k1] 18 (20) times, ssk, turn.
Repeat rows 2 and 3 until all side stitches have been worked; end having worked row 2. Turn your work and knit across, increasing 1 stitch evenly on this row. Needle 2 now holds 38 (42) stitches.

LEG

Work across needle 1 in the chart patterns.

Knitting the stitches off needle 2 onto the second of the larger circular needles, and making sure that you are starting on the same row of the charts as you are working on needle 1, work across the larger needle as follows: K1 tbl, work across the charts in the same manner as described for needle 1, k1 tbl.

You are now using both of the larger needles to knit the sock—you will not need the smaller needles again for this sock.

When your sock leg measures about 11" (28cm) from the bottom of the heel, or 1½" (3.8cm) shy of the desired leg length, ending after working an even row of the chart, work k1 tbl, p1 ribbing for 1½" (3.8cm). Bind off loosely in rib.

MANLY ARAN SOCKS

key

- K TBL
- P
- SL next stitch to cable needle, hold at back of work, K TBL the next stitch, and then P the stitch from the cable needle.
- SL next stitch to cable needle, hold at front of work, P the next stitch, and then K TBL the stitch from the cable needle.
- SL next stitch to cable needle, hold at back of work, K TBL the next stitch, and then K TBL the stitch from the cable needle.
- SL next stitch to cable needle, hold at front of work, K TBL the next stitch, and then K TBL the stitch from the cable needle.

chart a

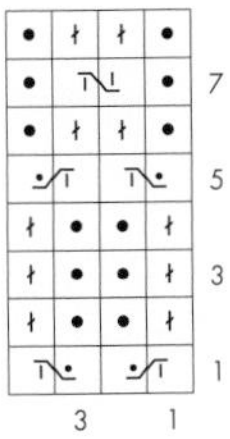

chart b

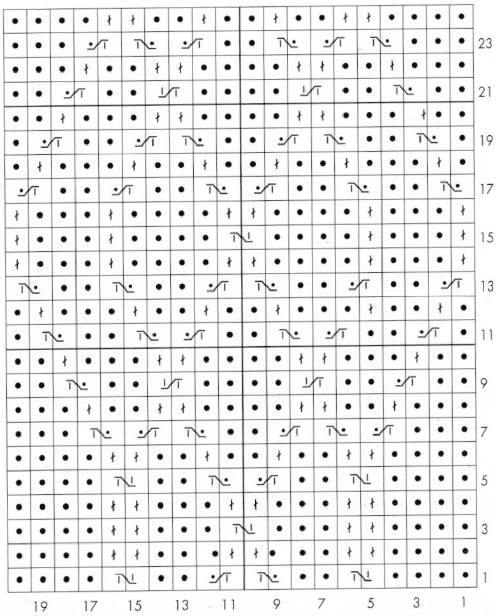

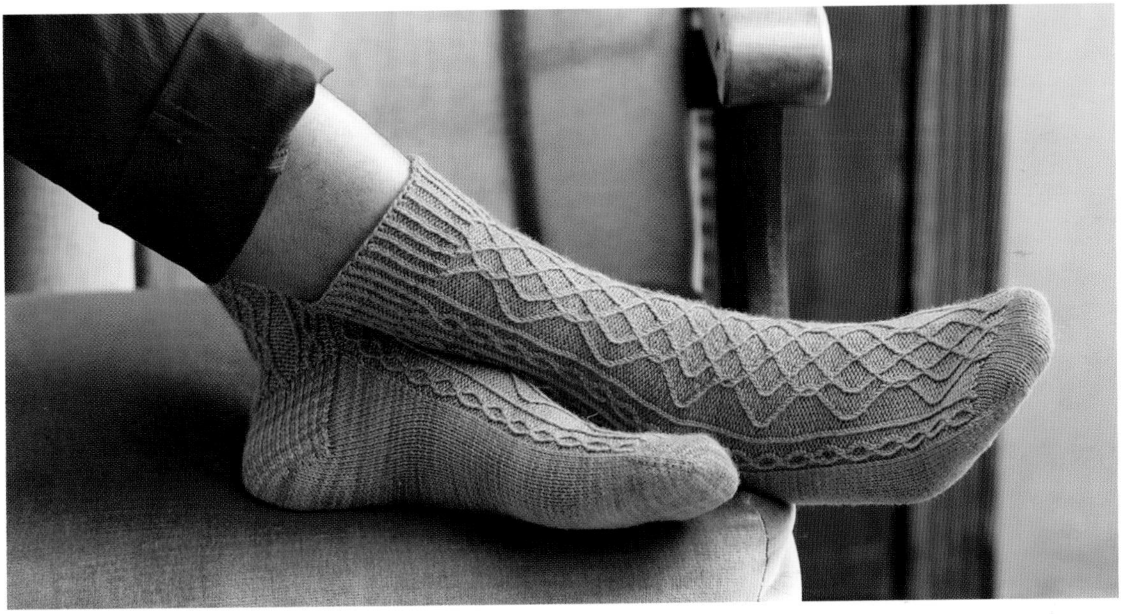

wrought iron socks and kneesocks

······································

I have always loved ornate wrought iron. I am in awe of the artisans who can take a material as hard and unyielding as iron and turn it into the gentle scrolls and filigree of a fence or an old-fashioned storm door. Naturally, I interpret these twists and turns as knitting stitches. The graceful curves of this cabled design are a tribute to the wrought iron I see in my mind's eye.

This design has two options: socks and kneesocks. To make the kneesocks, you incorporate an increase chart into the back of the leg and, of course, knit a longer leg.

SIZE
Socks S (M, L), 7 (8, 9)" (18 [20.5, 23]cm) circumference at foot, 9" (23cm) long foot, 11" (28cm) tall leg measured from the bottom of the foot to the top of the cuff.

Kneesocks S (M, L), 11 (12, 13)" (28 [30.5, 33]cm) circumference below the knee; 17" (43cm) tall leg measured from the bottom of the foot to the top of the cuff.

GAUGE 8 stitches and 12 rows = 1" (2.5cm) in stockinette stitch

NEEDLES 2 US size 0 (2mm) circular needles, or size needed to attain gauge, and 2 US size 1 (2.5mm) circular needles; cable needle

YARN
Socks (Kneesocks) 1 (2) skein(s) Cherry Tree Hill Supersock Solids, 100% luxury merino fingering weight, 4 oz (113.5g), 420 yd (384m), Turquoise, (**1**) Superfine

TOE

Using the smaller needles and a Turkish Cast-On, a Figure-Eight Cast-On, or Judy's Magic Cast-On, cast on a total of 26 (30, 34) stitches—13 (15, 17) stitches on each needle. Knit across the stitches on each needle once. On the next round, increase 4 stitches as follows:

Needle 1 K1, m1, knit until the last stitch, m1, k1.

Needle 2 K1, m1, knit until the last stitch, m1, k1.

Then knit a round without increasing.

Repeat these 2 rounds until you have a total of 58 (66, 74) stitches—29 (33, 37) stitches on each needle.

START THE CABLE PATTERN

You will work the Wrought Iron cable chart over needle 1 only (the instep stitches) and knit across needle 2 (the sole stitches).

Knit the stitches off needle 1 onto one of the larger circular needles as follows: P0 (1, 2), work the 14 stitches of row 1 of the cable chart, p0 (1, 2), k1 tbl, p0 (1, 2), work the 14 stitches of row 1 of the cable chart, p0 (1, 2).

Knit across the stitches on needle 2 (keeping the stitches on the smaller circular needle).

Continue in this manner, working as many repeats of the 38-row pattern as necessary until approximately 3" (7.5cm) shy of the total length of the foot.

CREATE THE GUSSET

Round 1 Work across needle 1 in the cable pattern. Needle 2 (sole stitches): K1, m1, knit across to the last stitch, m1, k1.

Round 2 Work across needle 1 in the cable pattern. Needle 2 (sole stitches): Knit all stitches.

Repeat rounds 1 and 2 until you have 49 (55, 61) stitches on needle 2. Work across needle 1 in the chart pattern.

TURN THE HEEL

You will now work back and forth on the stitches on needle 2 and will not knit the stitches on needle 1 while turning the heel. Turn the heel as follows:

Row 1 (RS) K33 (37, 41), kf&b, k1, w&t.

Row 2 P20 (22, 24), pf&b, p1, w&t.

Row 3 K18 (20, 22), kf&b, k1, w&t.

Row 4 P16 (18, 20), pf&b, p1, w&t.

Row 5 K14 (16, 18), kf&b, k1, w&t.

Row 6 P12 (14, 16), pf&b, p1, w&t.

Row 7 K10 (12, 14), kf&b, k1, w&t.

Row 8 P8 (10, 12), pf&b, p1, w&t.

Needle 2 now holds 57 (63, 69) stitches, having just completed a wrong-side row. On the right side, knit to the end of needle 2, knitting each wrap together with the stitch it wraps. Work across the instep stitches on needle 1 in the chart pattern.

HEEL FLAP

Work back and forth on the heel stitches on needle 2:

Row 1 (RS) K42 (47, 52) (knitting each wrap together with the stitch it wraps), ssk, turn.

Row 2 Sl1, p27 (31, 35), p2tog, turn.

Row 3 [Sl1, k1] 14 (16, 18) times, ssk, turn.

Repeat rows 2 and 3 until all side stitches have been worked; end having worked row 2. Turn your work and knit across, increasing 2 stitches evenly on this row. Needle 2 now holds 31 (35, 39) stitches.

LEG

Work across needle 1 in the cable chart pattern.

Knitting the stitches off needle 2 onto the second of the larger circular needles, and making sure that you are starting on the same row of the Wrought Iron chart as you are working on needle 1, work across the larger needle as follows: K1 tbl, work across the row in the same manner as described for needle 1, k1 tbl.

You are now using both of the larger needles to knit the sock—you will not need the smaller needles again for this sock.

Socks

Work the cable pattern. When your sock leg measures about 10" (25.5cm) from the bottom of the heel, or 1" (2.5cm) shy of the desired leg length, work in k1 tbl, p1 ribbing for 1" (2.5cm). Bind off very loosely in rib.

Kneesocks

Work the cable pattern for 6 rounds. On the seventh round, following the Wrought Iron increase chart, increase 1 stitch, knitwise, on each side of the center back stitch. Work even for 7 more rounds and then increase 1 stitch, purlwise, on each side of the center back stitch.

Continue in this manner, increasing 1 stitch, purlwise, on each side of the center back stitch until you have a total of 88 (96, 104) stitches—29 (33, 37) stitches on needle 1, and 59 (63, 67) stitches on needle 2. When your sock leg measures about 15" (38cm) from the bottom of the heel, or about 2" (5cm) shy of

the desired leg length, ending after working an even row of the chart, work k1 tbl, p1 ribbing for 2" (5cm). Bind off loosely in rib.

Note The increase chart shows the increases through row 40. Continue increasing in the same manner for a total of 14 times until you reach the correct number of stitches.

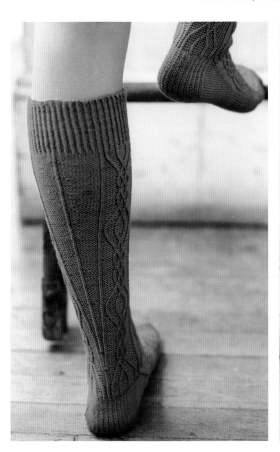 

TIP: MAKING LIFTED INCREASES NEATLY

There are many different techniques for m1, or make 1 increases. For a nonlace pattern that has increases on the leg (such as the Wrought Iron Kneesocks described here), I like to do lifted increases, which, if done carefully, result in an almost indiscernible hole in the fabric, preferable when you are knitting a "solid" rather than a lace design.

With the tip of your right-hand needle, pick up the strand of yarn in between the stitch you just knit and the stitch you are about to knit. Twist it and place it on the left-hand needle; then knit or purl as a new stitch.

ALL ABOUT KNEESOCKS

One of the biggest complaints I hear about kneesocks is that they have a tendency to fall down. How do you make kneesocks stay up without resorting to placing rubber bands around your cuffs or gluing them to your legs? The answer is sizing: Knit them to fit.

The Wrought Iron Kneesocks pattern is written to fit "average" legs, but of course there are many variations on either side of average. You want the leg to fit snugly—how snugly is really up to you, but it's best to aim for at least 1" (2.5cm) less than the actual circumference of the leg, perhaps 2" (5cm) for a nicely snug fit. To tailor the pattern to fit the leg perfectly, start by taking some key measurements of the recipient's legs. Measure the leg at several points: around the ankle, around the calf at the widest point, and halfway between the ankle and the widest point of the calf. How much wider the calf measurement is than the ankle will give you a general idea of how many times you should repeat the increase up to that widest point of the calf. If there is a difference of more than ½" (13mm) or so between the calf measurement and the knee measurement, you will want to work a couple of decreases back down to just below the knee.

Then measure the distance between the ankle and the widest point of the calf and the distance from the widest point of the calf to just below the knee. The distance measurements will, of course, also help you figure out how tall to make your sock. If you want the cuff to be part of the length of the sock to the knee, you need to take the depth of the cuff into consideration as part of the total length of the leg. If you plan to fold down the cuff, you don't have to think about it until you've knit the sock leg to the desired length. You must also remember that when the sock is worn, it will be shorter on the leg than it is when lying flat, because some of the length will be taken up as the sock is stretched to fit the width of the leg.

The most efficient way to get a great-fitting sock that is tall enough is to try it on as you knit. Knit the leg of the sock straight for a couple of inches (how many inches depends on the distance between the ankle and where the curve of the calf begins); then just slip it on. You can try on multiple times if need be. As you do so, it will become evident where the leg starts to swell out, and you'll be able to figure out exactly where you need to work the first increase. Make a note of how many rows you worked above the heel before the first increase. After you have knit for ½" to 1" (13mm to 2.5cm) after the first increase, try the sock on again to identify where you need the next increase. When you reach the point on the leg where the sock starts to feel snug, work the next pair of increases, and note how many rounds you have worked since the last increases.

Continue in this manner, trying on and increasing, until the sock is long enough to reach the widest point of the calf and fits comfortably but snugly around the calf. You will now knit until the sock reaches the desired height. If the measurement around your leg right below the knee is considerably smaller than the widest point of the calf, you will want to do a set or two of decreases spaced out over the distance between the widest point and the top of the sock.

CONVERTING A CABLE SOCK TO A KNEESOCK

You can use the Wrought Iron increase chart to adapt some of the other cabled socks in this book into kneesocks. You can use the increase chart almost "as is" with the Bob and Weave Socks (page 82), doing the increases on either side of the center purl stitch for the smaller size, and on either side of the twisted knit for the larger size. For the Basket Case Socks (page 86) and the Diamonds and Cables Socks (page 78), knit the increases on each side of the central motif. For a custom fit use the information above to knit your converted kneesock.

WROUGHT IRON SOCKS AND KNEESOCKS

key

⅄	K TBL
•	P
ㆁ	M1
⅄	Center stitch (worked K1 TBL)
■	No stitch
⅄T	SL next stitch to cable needle, hold at back of work, K TBL the next stitch, and then P the stitch from the cable needle.
T⅄	SL next stitch to cable needle, hold at front of work, P the next stitch, and then K TBL the stitch from the cable needle.
⅃T	SL next stitch to cable needle, hold at back of work, K TBL the next stitch, and then K TBL the stitch from the cable needle.
T⅃	SL next stitch to cable needle, hold at front of work, K TBL the next stitch, and then K TBL the stitch from the cable needle.

cable chart

increase chart

13 11 9 7 5 3 1

11 9 7 5 3 1

37 35 33 31 29 27 25 23 21 19 17 15 13 11 9 7 5 3 1

39 37 35 33 31 29 27 25 23 21 19 17 15 13 11 9 7 5 3 1

diamonds and cables socks

As I mentioned at the start of this chapter, I've been making fisherman knits since I was a teenager. One mainstay of Irish fisherman sweaters is the diamond motif, and it is a favorite of mine. This design has a wide panel centered on the front and back of the sock that creates a diamond with a small cable running down the center of the panel. This design is a departure from the traditional motif, however, because some unexpected lace stitches are added to the pattern along with the cable twists.

SIZE S (M, L), 7 (8, 9)" (18 [20.5, 23]cm) circumference, 9" (23cm) long foot, and 10" (25.5cm) tall leg measured from the bottom of the foot to the top of the cuff

GAUGE 8 stitches and 12 rows = 1" (2.5cm) in stockinette stitch

NEEDLES 2 US size 0 (2mm) circular needles, or size needed to attain gauge, and 2 US size 1 (2.5mm) circular needles; cable needle

YARN 1 skein Cherry Tree Hill Supersock Solids, 100% luxury merino fingering weight, 4 oz (113.5g), 420 yd (384m), Loden, (**1**) Superfine

TOE

Using the smaller needles and a Turkish Cast-On, a Figure-Eight Cast-On, or Judy's Magic Cast-On, cast on a total of 26 (30, 34) stitches—13 (15, 17) stitches on each needle. Knit across the stitches on each needle once. On the next round, increase 4 stitches as follows:

Needle 1 K1, m1, knit until the last stitch, m1, k1.

Needle 2 K1, m1, knit until the last stitch, m1, k1.

Then knit a round without increasing.

Repeat these 2 rounds until you have a total of 58 (66, 74) stitches—29 (33, 37) stitches on each needle.

START THE LACE AND CABLE PATTERN

You will work the charts over needle 1 only (the instep stitches) and knit across needle 2 (the sole stitches). Knitting the stitches off needle 1 onto one of the larger circular needles, work row 1 of the charts over the 29 (33, 37) stitches on needle 1 as follows: K1 (2, 3), work the 10 stitches of Diamonds and Cables chart A, k0 (1, 2), work the 7 stitches of Diamonds and Cables chart B, k0 (1, 2), work the 10 stitches of Diamonds and Cables chart C, k1 (2, 3).

Knit across the stitches on needle 2 (keeping the stitches on the smaller circular needle).

Continue in this manner, working as many repeats of the 20-row chart A and chart C patterns and the 10-row chart B pattern as necessary until approximately 3" (7.5cm) shy of the total length of the foot.

CREATE THE GUSSET

Round 1 Work across needle 1 in pattern. Needle 2 (sole stitches): K1, m1, knit across to the last stitch, m1, k1.

Round 2 Work across needle 1 in pattern. Needle 2 (sole stitches): Knit all stitches.

Repeat rounds 1 and 2 until you have 49 (55, 61) stitches on needle 2. Work across needle 1 in the chart patterns.

TURN THE HEEL

You will now work back and forth on the stitches on needle 2 and will not knit the stitches on needle 1 while turning the heel. Turn the heel as follows:

Row 1 (RS) K33 (37, 41), kf&b, k1, w&t.

Row 2 P20 (22, 24), pf&b, p1, w&t.

Row 3 K18 (20, 22), kf&b, k1, w&t.

Row 4 P16 (18, 20), pf&b, p1, w&t.

Row 5 K14 (16, 18), kf&b, k1, w&t.

Row 6 P12 (14, 16), pf&b, p1, w&t.

Row 7 K10 (12, 14), kf&b, k1, w&t.

Row 8 P8 (10, 12), pf&b, p1, w&t.

Needle 2 now holds 57 (63, 69) stitches, having just completed a wrong-side row. On the right side, knit to the end of needle 2, knitting each wrap together with the stitch it wraps. Work across the instep stitches on needle 1 in the chart patterns.

HEEL FLAP

Work back and forth on the heel stitches on needle 2:

Row 1 (RS) K42 (47, 52) (knitting each wrap together with the stitch it wraps), ssk, turn.

Row 2 Sl1, p27 (31, 35), p2tog, turn.

Row 3 [Sl1, k1] 14 (16, 18) times, ssk, turn.

Repeat rows 2 and 3 until all side stitches have been worked; end having worked row 2. Turn your work and knit across.

LEG

Work across needle 1 in the chart patterns.

Knitting the stitches off needle 2 onto the second of the larger circular needles, and making sure that you are starting on the same row of the charts as you are working on needle 1, work across the larger needle in the same manner as described for needle 1. You are now using both of the larger needles to knit the sock—you will not need the smaller needles again for this sock.

When your sock leg measures about 9" (23cm) from the bottom of the heel, or 1" (2.5cm) shy of the desired leg length, work in k1, p1 ribbing for 1" (2.5cm). Bind off very loosely in rib.

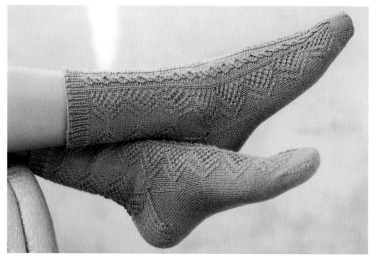
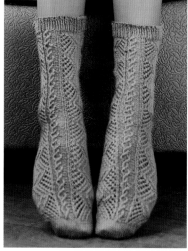

DIAMONDS AND CABLES SOCKS

key

	K
ɬ	K TBL
•	P
O	YO
/	K2TOG
\	SSK
✕	SL next stitch to cable needle, hold at back of work, K the next stitch, and then K the stitch from the cable needle.
✕	SL next stitch to cable needle, hold at front of work, K the next stitch, and then K the stitch from the cable needle.
⌐T	SL next stitch to cable needle, hold at back of work, K TBL the next stitch, and then P the stitch from the cable needle.
T⌐	SL next stitch to cable needle, hold at front of work, P the next stitch, and then K TBL the stitch from the cable needle.
⊥ ⊥ ⌐	SL next 2 stitches to cable needle, hold at back of work, K TBL the next stitch, move the second stitch from the cable needle to the left needle, P the next stitch, and then K TBL the stitch from the cable needle.

chart a

chart b

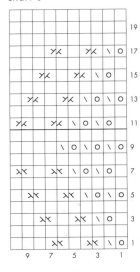

chart c

bob and weave socks

....

I am fascinated by braided and woven patterns—the more complex the better! As a teenager, I could often be found in front of a mirror, braiding my hair in a six- or seven-strand French braid. While I do still sometimes French-braid my hair, I'm now more likely to put complex braids in my knitting. Because these socks have a heavily cabled, allover design, you might need to go up another needle size on the cabled portions if you are knitting for a leg that is more shapely than slender. The cable twists are worked on every row, so you will need to stay alert as you knit.

SIZE M (L), 8 (9)" (20.5 [23]cm) circumference, 9" (23cm) long foot, and 9" (23cm) tall leg measured from the bottom of the foot to the top of the cuff

GAUGE 8 stitches and 12 rows = 1" (2.5cm) in stockinette stitch

NEEDLES 2 US size 0 (2mm) circular needles, or size needed to attain gauge, and 2 US size 1 (2.5mm) circular needles; cable needle

YARN 2 (3) skeins Artyarns Ultramerino 4, 100% merino wool, 1¾ oz (50g), 191 yd (174.5m), Gold (#231), **1** Superfine

TOE
Using the smaller needles and a Turkish Cast-On, a Figure-Eight Cast-On, or Judy's Magic Cast-On, cast on a total of 30 (34) stitches—15 (17) stitches on each needle. Knit across the stitches on each needle once. On the next round, increase 4 stitches as follows:

Needle 1 K1, m1, knit until the last stitch, m1, k1.

Needle 2 K1, m1, knit until the last stitch, m1, k1.

Then knit a round without increasing.

Repeat these 2 rounds until you have a total of 66 (74) stitches—33 (37) stitches on each needle.

START THE CABLE PATTERN
You will work the Bob and Weave cable chart over needle 1 only (the instep stitches) and knit across needle 2 (the sole stitches). Knitting the stitches off needle 1 onto one of the larger circular needles, work row 1 of the chart as follows:

For size M

Work the cable chart over the next 16 stitches, p1, work the cable chart over the next 16 stitches (33 stitches total on needle 1).

For size L

P1, work the cable chart over the next 16 stitches, p1, k1 tbl, p1, work the cable chart over the next 16 stitches, p1 (37 stitches total on needle 1).

For both sizes

Knit across the stitches on needle 2 (keeping the stitches on the smaller circular needle).

Continue in this manner, working as many repeats of the 14-row pattern as necessary until approximately 3" (7.5cm) shy of the total length of the foot.

CREATE THE GUSSET

Round 1 Work across needle 1 in the cable pattern. Needle 2 (sole stitches): K1, m1, knit across to the last stitch, m1, k1.

Round 2 Work across needle 1 in the cable pattern. Needle 2 (sole stitches): Knit all stitches.

Repeat rounds 1 and 2 until you have 55 (61) stitches on needle 2. Work across needle 1 in the cable pattern.

TURN THE HEEL

You will now work back and forth on the stitches on needle 2 and will not knit the stitches on needle 1 while turning the heel. Turn the heel as follows:

Row 1 (RS) K37 (41), kf&b, k1, w&t.
Row 2 P22 (24), pf&b, p1, w&t.
Row 3 K20 (22), kf&b, k1, w&t.
Row 4 P18 (20), pf&b, p1, w&t.
Row 5 K16 (18), kf&b, k1, w&t.
Row 6 P14 (16), pf&b, p1, w&t.
Row 7 K12 (14), kf&b, k1, w&t.
Row 8 P10 (12), pf&b, p1, w&t.
Needle 2 now holds 63 (69) stitches, having just completed a wrong-side row. On the right side, knit to the end of needle 2, knitting each wrap together with the stitch it wraps. Work across the instep stitches on needle 1 in the chart pattern.

HEEL FLAP

Work back and forth on the heel stitches on needle 2:
Row 1 (RS) K47 (52) (knitting each wrap together with the stitch it wraps), ssk, turn.
Row 2 Sl1, p31 (35), p2tog, turn.
Row 3 [Sl1, k1] 16 (18) times, ssk, turn.
Repeat rows 2 and 3 until all side stitches have been worked; end having worked row 2. Turn your work and knit across, increasing 2 stitches evenly on this row. Needle 2 now holds 35 (39) stitches.

LEG

Work across needle 1 in the chart pattern.

Knitting the stitches off needle 2 onto the second of the larger circular needles, and making sure that you are starting on the same row of the chart as you are working on needle 1, work across the larger needle as follows:

For size M

P1, work across the chart in the same manner as described for needle 1, p1.

For size L

K1 tbl, work across the chart in the same manner as described for needle 1, k1 tbl.

You are now using both of the larger needles to knit the sock—you will not need the smaller needles again for this sock.

When your sock leg measures about 8" (20.5cm) from the bottom of the heel, or 1" (2.5cm) shy of the desired leg length, ending after working an even row of the chart, work k1 tbl, p1 ribbing for 1" (2.5cm). Bind off loosely in rib.

BOB AND WEAVE SOCKS

key

ⱡ	K TBL
•	P
•／T	SL next stitch to cable needle, hold at back of work, K TBL the next stitch, and then P the stitch from the cable needle.
T＼•	SL next stitch to cable needle, hold at front of work, P the next stitch, and then K TBL the stitch from the cable needle.
↓／T	SL next stitch to cable needle, hold at back of work, K TBL the next stitch, and then K TBL the stitch from the cable needle.
T＼↓	SL next stitch to cable needle, hold at front of work, K TBL the next stitch, and then K TBL the stitch from the cable needle.

cable chart

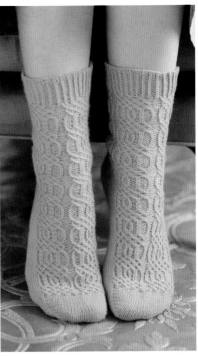

basket case socks

· ·

These socks feature some intricate cabling. A nontraditional basket-weave design forms a traditional diamond shape on either side of mirror-image center cables. There are cable twists on every row, so this is another "pay attention as you knit" pattern. And like the Bob and Weave Socks (page 82), you might want to go up another needle size on the cabled portions to accommodate a shapely leg. You'll want to use a solid color yarn for these socks—the lighter the color you use, the more striking the effect.

SIZE S (M, L), 7 (8, 9)" (18 [20.5, 23]cm) circumference, 9" (23cm) long foot, and 10" (25.5cm) tall leg measured from the bottom of the foot to the top of the cuff

GAUGE 8 stitches and 12 rows = 1" (2.5cm) in stockinette stitch

NEEDLES 2 US size 0 (2mm) circular needles, or size needed to attain gauge, and 2 US size 1 (2.5mm) circular needles; cable needle

YARN 2 skeins Lorna's Laces Shepherd Sock, 80% superwash wool and 20% nylon, 2 oz (56.5g), 215 yd (196.5m), Chino, (**1**) Superfine

TOE

Using the smaller needles and a Turkish Cast-On, a Figure-Eight Cast-On, or Judy's Magic Cast-On, cast on a total of 26 (30, 34) stitches—13 (15, 17) stitches on each needle. Knit across the stitches on each needle once. On the next round, increase 4 stitches as follows:

Needle 1 K1, m1, knit until the last stitch, m1, k1.

Needle 2 K1, m1, knit until the last stitch, m1, k1.

Then knit a round without increasing.

Repeat these 2 rounds until

you have a total of 58 (66, 74) stitches—29 (33, 37) stitches on each needle.

START THE CABLE PATTERN

You will work the Basket Case cable chart over needle 1 only (the instep stitches) and knit across needle 2 (the sole stitches).

Knitting the stitches off needle 1 onto one of the larger circular needles, work row 1 of the cable chart over the 29 (33, 37) stitches on needle 1. Knit across stitches on needle 2 (keeping the stitches on the smaller circular needle). Continue in this manner, working as

many repeats of the 20-row pattern as necessary until approximately 3" (7.5cm) shy of the total length of the foot.

CREATE THE GUSSET

Round 1 Work across needle 1 in the cable pattern. Needle 2 (sole stitches): K1, m1, knit across to the last stitch, m1, k1.

Round 2 Work across needle 1 in the cable pattern. Needle 2 (sole stitches): Knit all stitches.

Repeat rounds 1 and 2 until you have 49 (55, 61) stitches on needle 2. Work across needle 1 in the chart pattern.

TURN THE HEEL

You will now work back and forth on the stitches on needle 2 and will not knit the stitches on needle 1 while turning the heel. Turn the heel as follows:

Row 1 (RS) K33 (37, 41), kf&b, k1, w&t.

Row 2 P20 (22, 24), pf&b, p1, w&t.

Row 3 K18 (20, 22), kf&b, k1, w&t.

Row 4 P16 (18, 20), pf&b, p1, w&t.

Row 5 K14 (16, 18), kf&b, k1, w&t.

Row 6 P12 (14, 16), pf&b, p1, w&t.

Row 7 K10 (12, 14), kf&b, k1, w&t.

Row 8 P8 (10, 12), pf&b, p1, w&t.

Needle 2 now holds 57 (63, 69) stitches, having just completed a wrong-side row. On the right side, knit to the end of needle 2, knitting each wrap together with the stitch it wraps. Work across the instep stitches on needle 1 in the chart pattern.

HEEL FLAP

Work back and forth on the heel stitches on needle 2:

Row 1 (RS) K42 (47, 52) (knitting each wrap together with the stitch it wraps), ssk, turn.

Row 2 Sl1, p27 (31, 35), p2tog, turn.

Row 3 [Sl1, k1] 14 (16, 18) times, ssk, turn.

Repeat rows 2 and 3 until all side stitches have been worked; end having worked row 2. Turn your work and knit across, increasing 2 stitches evenly on this row. Needle 2 now holds 31 (35, 39) stitches.

LEG

Work across needle 1 in the chart pattern.

Knitting the stitches off needle 2 onto the second of the larger circular needles, and making sure that you are starting on the same row of the chart as you are working on needle 1, work across the larger needle as follows: K1 tbl, work across the cable chart in the same manner as described for needle 1, k1 tbl.

You are now using both of the larger needles to knit the sock—you will not need the smaller needles again for this sock.

When your sock leg measures about 9" (23cm) from the bottom of the heel, or 1" (2.5cm) shy of the desired leg length, ending after working an even row of the chart, work k1 tbl, p1 ribbing for 1" (2.5cm). Bind off loosely in rib.

BASKET CASE SOCKS

key

☐	K
ꜰ	K TBL
•	P

⧓ — SL next stitch to cable needle, hold at back of work, K the next stitch, and then K the stitch from the cable needle.

⧓ — SL next stitch to cable needle, hold at front of work, K the next stitch, and then K the stitch from the cable needle.

⧓ — SL next stitch to cable needle, hold at back of work, K TBL the next stitch, and then K TBL the stitch from the cable needle.

⧓ — SL next stitch to cable needle, hold at front of work, K TBL the next stitch, and then K TBL the stitch from the cable needle.

⧓ — SL next stitch to cable needle, hold at back of work, K TBL the next stitch, and then P the stitch from the cable needle.

⧓ — SL next stitch to cable needle, hold at front of work, P the next stitch, and then K TBL the stitch from the cable needle.

small cable chart

medium cable chart

large cable chart

COLORWORK SOCKS

There are basically two types of
colorwork: intarsia and stranded.
To work intarsia, you keep each
"block" of color separate and usually
use bobbins for each color section,
twisting the two colors together at the
edges of sections where they meet.
In stranded colorwork, you knit with
two colors and carry the color not
in use along the back of your work
while you knit with the other color.
All of the colorwork socks here are
created by stranding and use only
two colors at a time.

the colorwork patterns at a glance

This chart lists all of the patterns in this section, the special stitches used in each, and my assessment of their difficulty. Instructions for all necessary techniques and some useful tips are provided in the Colorwork Techniques section (page 92).

LEVEL	PATTERN	TECHNIQUE
✳	Sneaky Argyle Socks	colorwork on leg only
✳✳	Stjärnblommesockor	colorwork on leg only, uses 3 colors
✳✳	Critter Socks	colorwork on leg only, uses 3 colors
✳✳✳	Sanquhar Socks	allover colorwork, corrugated ribbing
✳✳✳	Norwegian Rose Socks	allover colorwork, corrugated ribbing
✳✳✳	Fair Isle Socks	allover colorwork
✳✳✳	Hot Stuff! Socks	"free-form" colorwork

Typically when knitting stranded colorwork, the unused color carried along the wrong side of your work is "woven" in; the yarn not in use is twisted with the working yarn every 2 or 3 stitches on the wrong side to catch it and hold it in place. However, colorwork socks demand their own consideration. I *strongly* recommend that you let that yarn "float"—simply ignore the yarn not in use until it is time to use it again and then just pick it up and knit with it. I almost always float, even for stretches as significant as 10 stitches. As long as I don't let the stitches bunch up on the needle, I have no problem with tension. And as I knit, I take care that the floating yarn stretches out properly so that the knitting doesn't pucker when I pick up to knit the floating yarn. The only drawback I've found to floating colorwork is occasionally catching a toe in a long float when putting a sock on my foot!

There are a couple of reasons for floating in colorwork. First, I find that weaving sometimes shows on the right side, particularly when using very fine yarns, such as sock yarns. Also, weaving the color not in use makes the fabric firmer and far less stretchy. A firm, nonstretchy fabric may be good for a cardigan, but it is something you definitely don't want when you are knitting socks. If you have woven your colorwork, you will be hard-pressed to actually put the sock on. If, by some Herculean effort, you do manage to get the sock on the foot, you will find that the woven fabric will not allow the sock to shape itself nicely against your foot and leg: The curve of ankle to heel will not be discernible in your very firm, unyielding sock.

Another consideration when you are knitting colorwork socks is how you work the heel. My favorite heel, the slip stitch heel, is worked back and forth on only the heel stitches for the most part, but there are points in the heel construction where you need to work around the circumference of the sock. This is a problem when you are knitting with two colors, because the heel is worked in one color only. The foreground color will be left hanging at the end of the instep stitches when you are back at the start of the round. You could break the foreground color and reattach it to work the couple of complete rounds you need to work for the heel, but I prefer to use a heel whose creation does not require any work on the instep stitches. So, for the allover colorwork socks, I've devised a short-row heel with mini gusset (page 137). The mini gusset and heel flap adds a bit of extra room in the sock to counteract the less stretchy colorwork fabric.

COLORWORK TECHNIQUES

Now that I have frightened you enough so that you won't even consider weaving your colorwork, we can take a look at some of the essential techniques for successful color knitting.

Stranding There are different ways to hold your yarn for doing two-color knitting. If you are new to colorwork, experiment to find the way that works best for you. Your preferred stranding technique will probably be influenced by which hand you use to wrap your yarn as you knit (English, Continental, and so forth) and your "handedness." No matter which method you use, be sure that you always work your colors in the same order—that is, always keep the foreground color on top and the background color on the bottom. If you mix them up, you will see subtle differences in your knitted fabric. Also remember that there is really no wrong way to hold your yarn, as long as you get the results you want.

• **holding colors in the left hand** If you are a lefty, like me, and/or a Continental knitter, try holding both colors in your left hand. I prefer to hold both yarns over my index finger, with a bit of space between the two strands. However, if two strands over one finger is too fiddly for you, try holding one color over the index finger and another over the middle finger. You will knit with the desired strand by "picking" in the Continental style. **(a)**

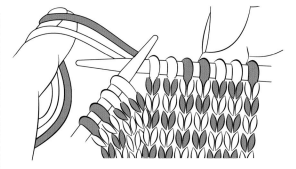

(a) holding colors in the left hand

When you hold both colors in your left hand, you can also employ a little doodad called a *strickfingerhut*, or "knitting thimble." This device slips over the index finger on your left hand with each color threaded through a guide. I've never had success with this gadget as I find myself dropping and picking up yarns a lot, but some people use it with success.

• **holding colors in each hand**
If you are more ambidextrous than I and have no problem wrapping stitches with either hand, try holding one color in each hand. You will knit with the yarn in the left hand by picking, in the Continental style, and knit with the yarn in the right hand by throwing the yarn, in the English style. **(b)**

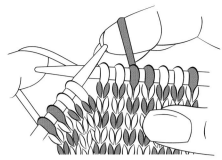

(b) holding colors in each hand

I was taught this method years ago in a Norwegian knitting class and can attest to its speed and elegance. However, being profoundly left-handed (and profoundly stubborn), I returned to my familiar method of holding both yarns in my left hand. I encourage you to be less unyielding than I am, though, and give this a try.

• holding colors in the right hand

If you have a strong preference for using your right hand or are an English knitter, you can hold both colors in your right hand. You knit both strands by wrapping in the English method. If you hold both yarns in your right hand, I find the easiest way is to pinch both colors between index finger and thumb and simply knit with the appropriate color. But, of course, you'll want to hold the yarns in a manner that is comfortable for you. **(c)**

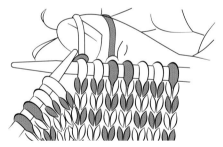

(c) holding colors in the right hand

Tension for Colorwork Socks As you work stranded knitting, you need to remain aware of your tension. If your floats are too short, you'll end up with a sock that has little stretch; if your floats are too loose, you'll have gaps between your two colors.

For even tension, spread your stitches out as you knit so that they are lying naturally, as they would when off the needle. I find that this is easiest to do if you use needles that have a bit of "grab" to them, such as wooden needles. If you do this, the float across the back of your work will be the correct length, your stitches will be uniform, and your knitted fabric will lie smooth.

Some people find that turning their work inside out helps their tension. You will knit inside the tube— the right side of your work—and carry the floats along the outside of the tube. Because the outside circumference of the sock is slightly larger than the inside circumference, your floats will be slightly longer and therefore less likely to create a stiff, puckered finished fabric.

As you knit, don't be alarmed if your colorwork looks slightly bumpy as it comes off the needles. This is to be expected. Rare is the knitter who can knit perfectly smooth colorwork without blocking it! You'll be surprised and pleased to see how many lumps and bumps disappear once you soak your socks in warm water and pop them on sock blockers to dry.

Working Corrugated Ribbing Often used in color knitting, corrugated ribbing is done by working the knit stitches in one color and the purl stitches in another color. It is by nature tighter than "regular" ribbing, so take care to work it loosely or work it using a larger needle.

For a k2, p2 ribbing:
Knit 2 with color A. **(d)**

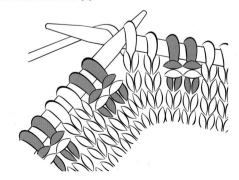

(d) corrugated ribbing

Move color B to the front. **(e)**

Purl 2 with color B. **(f)**

Move color B to the back. Knit 2 with color A. **(g)**

Repeat this around, until your ribbing is as long as you desire. While a two-color bind-off is attractive with corrugated ribbing, it will probably be too tight for binding off a sock cuff. I prefer to bind off loosely in one color when I'm working a corrugated ribbing on socks.

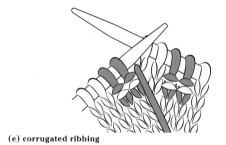

(e) corrugated ribbing

(f) corrugated ribbing

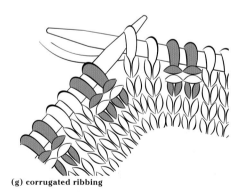

(g) corrugated ribbing

Working Duplicate Stitch

Duplicate stitch, also called "swiss darning," is used either to add decoration or to cover up mistakes on a knitted fabric. You work it on the surface of your knitting fabric with yarn threaded through a round-tip tapestry needle.

Bring the needle through from the back of the sock to the front through the base of the stitch to be covered. Then insert the needle from right to left behind the stitch directly above. **(h)** Next, insert the needle from front to back into the base of the stitch you want to cover and gently pull the yarn through to the back so that you've completely covered the "V" of the stitch with the new yarn. **(i)**

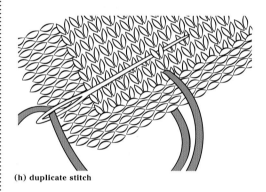

(h) duplicate stitch

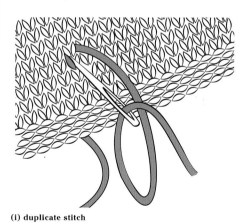

(i) duplicate stitch

If you keep the tension the same as the knitted fabric, no one will ever know that you have duplicate stitched over your knitting—unless they are looking very closely at your work. **(j)**

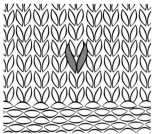

(j) duplicate stitch

Weaving in Ends When you are working on more than one color, you'll have multiple ends to deal with when you finish your sock. Using a round-tip tapestry needle, weave like colors together—for example, weave a black end

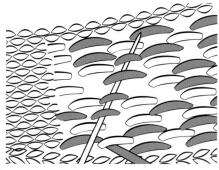

(k) weaving in ends

through black stitches and a white end through white stitches—through purl bumps on the wrong side of the sock. **(k)**

When weaving in ends, make sure to maintain the same tension as your knitting. I find it helpful to weave for about 1½" (3.8cm) on a diagonal, and then tug on the fabric gently before trimming the woven end. This relaxes the end and ensures that it hasn't been pulled too tightly. **(l)**

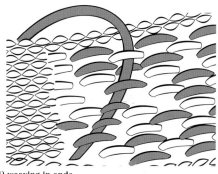

(l) weaving in ends

YARNS FOR COLORWORK SOCKS

With colorwork, you can go a little wild and have fun with your yarn choices! While most of the sample socks here are knit with solid or semisolid colors, you could experiment by knitting a design with a solid background and a variegated foreground. This works beautifully as long as there is enough contrast between the two yarns to make the design stand out. I find that variegated yarns can be duplicitous. It may look mild-mannered and innocuous enough in the skein, but once you start knitting with it you may discover that it stripes or pools in a nefarious fashion. Therefore, it's a good idea to knit a swatch if you plan to let your colorwork go wild.

sneaky argyle socks

....

Classic argyle socks are knit using the intarsia technique. The leg of the sock is worked flat and seamed up the back after knitting. I loathe anything that requires extra work, so my argyles are sneaky: They are knit stranded. This pattern is a good place to start if you are new to colorwork, because the foot is knit in one color and the two-color portion does not start until after you turn the heel. Also, the simple geometric design, perfect for men and women, is easy to follow.

SIZE
Women's S (M, L, XL), 7 (8, 9, 10)" (18 [20.5, 23, 25.5]cm) circumference, 9" (23cm) long foot, and 9" (23cm) tall leg measured from the bottom of the foot to the top of the cuff

Men's XS (S, M, L), 7 (8, 9, 10)" (18 [20.5, 23, 25.5]cm) circumference, 10" (25.5cm) long foot, and 11" (28cm) tall leg measured from the bottom of the foot to the top of the cuff

GAUGE 8 stitches and 12 rows = 1" (2.5cm) in stockinette stitch on US size 0 (2mm) needles using 1 color; 8 stitches and 10 rows = 1" (2.5cm) in stockinette stitch on US size 1 (2.5mm) needles in colorwork pattern

NEEDLES 2 US size 0 (2mm) and 2 US size 1 (2.5mm) circular needles (or 1 long circular needle each), or sizes needed to attain gauge

YARN Louet Gems Fingering, 100% merino wool, 1¾ oz (50g), 185 yd (169m), 2 (2, 2, 3) skeins color A, 1 (1, 1, 2) skeins color B, **1** Superfine

Women's Seaspray (color A), Violet (color B)

Men's Steel Grey (color A), Burgundy (color B)

TOE
With color A and smaller needles, and using a Turkish Cast-On, a Figure-Eight Cast-On, or Judy's Magic Cast-On, cast on a total of 28 (32, 36, 40) stitches—14 (16, 18, 20) stitches on each needle. Knit across the stitches on each needle

once. On the next round, increase 4 stitches as follows:
Needle 1 K1, m1, knit until the last stitch, m1, k1.
Needle 2 K1, m1, knit until the last stitch, m1, k1.
Then knit a round without increasing.

Repeat these 2 rounds until you have a total of 56 (64, 72, 80) stitches—28 (32, 36, 40) stitches on each needle.
Knit in stockinette stitch (knit every round) until approximately 3" (7.5cm) shy of the total length of the foot.

CREATE THE GUSSET

Round 1 Knit across needle 1. Needle 2 (sole stitches): K1, m1, knit across to the last stitch, m1, k1.

Round 2 Knit all stitches. Repeat rounds 1 and 2 until you have 48 (54, 60, 66) stitches total on needle 2. On the last round, increase 1 stitch in the center of the sole (needle 2) for a total of 49 (55, 61, 67) stitches. Work across needle 1.

TURN THE HEEL

You will work back and forth on the stitches on needle 2 and will not knit the stitches on needle 1 while turning the heel. Turn the heel as follows:

Row 1 (RS) K33 (37, 41, 45), kf&b, k1, w&t.

Row 2 P20 (22, 24, 26), pf&b, p1, w&t.

Row 3 K18 (20, 22, 24), kf&b, k1, w&t.

Row 4 P16 (18, 20, 22), pf&b, p1, w&t.

Row 5 K14 (16, 18, 20), kf&b, k1, w&t.

Row 6 P12 (14, 16, 18), pf&b, p1, w&t.

Row 7 K10 (12, 14, 16), kf&b, k1, w&t.

Row 8 P8 (10, 12, 14), pf&b, p1, w&t.

Needle 2 now holds 57 (63, 69, 75) stitches, having just completed a wrong-side row. On the right side, knit to the end of needle 2, knitting each wrap together with the stitch it wraps. Knit across the instep stitches on needle 1.

HEEL FLAP

Work back and forth on the stitches on needle 2:

Row 1 (RS) K42 (47, 52, 57) (knitting each wrap together with the stitch it wraps), ssk, turn.

Row 2 Sl1, p27 (31, 35, 39), p2tog, turn.

Row 3 [Sl1, k1] 14 (16, 18, 20) times, ssk, turn.

Repeat rows 2 and 3 until all side stitches have been worked; end having worked row 2. Turn your work and knit across, decreasing 1 stitch in the center of the row. Needle 2 now holds 28 (32, 36, 40) stitches.

LEG

Begin working in the round again.

Start the Colorwork Pattern
Change to the larger-sized needles and work row 1 of the Sneaky Argyles colorwork chart. You will work row 1 four times: twice across needle 1 and twice across needle 2. Work the 14 (16, 18, 20) rows of the chart in this manner, repeating the chart 2 more times, for a total of 42 (48, 54, 60) rows worked; then break off color B. Knit 1 round plain in color A.

Using color A only, work 2" (5cm) in k1, p1 ribbing. Bind off loosely in rib.

SNEAKY ARGYLE SOCKS

key
☐ Color A
■ Color B

extra small colorwork chart

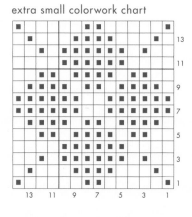

small colorwork chart

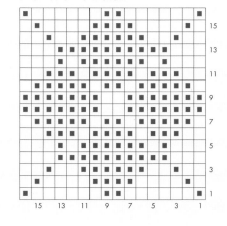

medium colorwork chart

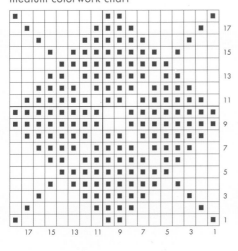

large colorwork chart

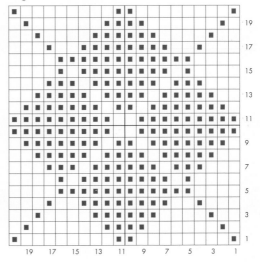

stjärnblommesockor

I am half Swedish and grew up surrounded by Swedish culture, crafts, and traditions—including knitting traditions. It's no wonder I wanted to create a Swedish design to celebrate my heritage. The name of this pattern translates to "Star Flower Socks," and the flower motif and colors used are reminiscent of traditional Swedish knitting. Because my Swedish friend Johanne Ländin named this pattern and suggested the colors I used, I naturally bullied her into knitting the sample socks for the book. This is another design that is good for a knitter new to colorwork, as the sock is knit in one color until you get to the cuff at the top of the leg.

SIZE S (M, L), 7 (8, 9)" (18 [20.5, 23]cm) circumference, 9" (23cm) long foot, and 9½" (24cm) tall leg measured from the bottom of the foot to the top of the cuff

GAUGE 8 stitches and 12 rows = 1" (2.5cm) in stockinette stitch on US size 0 (2mm) needles using 1 color; 8 stitches and 10 rows = 1" (2.5cm) in stockinette stitch on US size 1 (2.5mm) needles in colorwork pattern

NEEDLES 2 US size 0 (2mm) and 2 US size 1 (2.5mm) circular needles (or 1 long circular needle each), or sizes needed to attain gauge

YARN Cherry Tree Hill Supersock Solids, 100% luxury merino fingering weight, 4 oz (113.5g), 420 yd (384m), 1 skein Black (color A), approximately 25 yd (23m) Cherry (color B), approximately 25 yd (23m) Pesto (color C), **1** Superfine

TOE

With color A and the smaller needles, and using a Turkish Cast-On, a Figure-Eight Cast-On, or Judy's Magic Cast-On, cast on a total of 28 (32, 36) stitches—14 (16, 18) stitches on each needle. Knit across the stitches on each needle once. On the next round, increase 4 stitches as follows:

Needle 1 K1, m1, knit until the last stitch, m1, k1.

Needle 2 K1, m1, knit until the last stitch, m1, k1.
Then knit a round without increasing.
Repeat these 2 rounds until you have a total of 56 (64, 72) stitches—28 (32, 36) stitches on each needle.
Knit in stockinette stitch (knit every round) until approximately 3" (7.5cm) shy of the total length of the foot.

CREATE THE GUSSET

Round 1 Knit across needle 1.
Needle 2 (sole stitches): K1, m1, knit across to the last stitch, m1, k1.
Round 2 Knit all stitches.
Repeat rounds 1 and 2 until you have 48 (54, 60) stitches total on needle 2. On the last round, increase 1 stitch in the center of the sole (needle 2) for a total of 49 (55, 61) stitches. Work across needle 1.

TURN THE HEEL

You will work back and forth on the stitches on needle 2 and will not knit the stitches on needle 1 while turning the heel. Turn the heel as follows:

Row 1 (RS) K33 (37, 41), kf&b, k1, w&t.

Row 2 P20 (22, 24), pf&b, p1, w&t.

Row 3 K18 (20, 22), kf&b, k1, w&t.

Row 4 P16 (18, 20), pf&b, p1, w&t.

Row 5 K14 (16, 18), kf&b, k1, w&t.

Row 6 P12 (14, 16), pf&b, p1, w&t.

Row 7 K10 (12, 14), kf&b, k1, w&t.

Row 8 P8 (10, 12), pf&b, p1, w&t.

Needle 2 now holds 57 (63, 69) stitches, having just completed a wrong-side row. On the right side, knit to the end of needle 2, knitting each wrap together with the stitch it wraps. Work across the instep stitches on needle 1.

HEEL FLAP

Work back and forth on the stitches on needle 2:

Row 1 (RS) K42 (47, 52) (knitting each wrap together with the stitch it wraps), ssk, turn.

Row 2 Sl1, p27 (31, 35), p2tog, turn.

Row 3 [Sl1, k1] 14 (16, 18) times, ssk, turn.

Repeat rows 2 and 3 until all side stitches have been worked; end having worked row 2. Turn your work and knit across, decreasing 1 stitch in the center of the row. Needle 2 now holds 28 (32, 36) stitches.

LEG

Begin working in the round again. Work in stockinette stitch until your sock measures approximately 6" (15cm) from the bottom of the heel, or 3½" (9cm) shy of the desired leg length.

Start the Colorwork Pattern

Change to the larger-sized needles and work row 1 of the Stjärnblommesockor colorwork chart. You will work row 1 twice: once across needle 1 and once across needle 2.

Work all 22 rows of the chart in this manner; then work rows 1–8 again. Break off colors B and C and knit 5 rounds in color A.

Work a picot edge

Next round: K2tog, yo around all 56 (64, 72) stitches.

Knit 5 rounds to form a hem, and bind off very loosely. Leave a yarn tail of about 15" (38cm). Fold the hem to the inside of the sock (it will fold naturally along the round with the yarn overs), and loosely sew it to the inside of the sock using a tapestry needle and the yarn tail.

STJÄRNBLOMMESOCKOR

key

- ☐ Color A
- ■ Color B
- • Color C

small colorwork chart

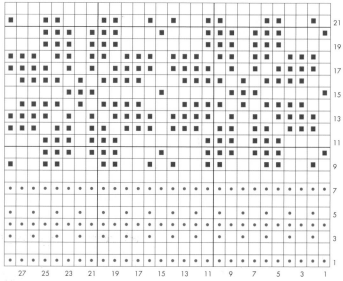

medium colorwork chart

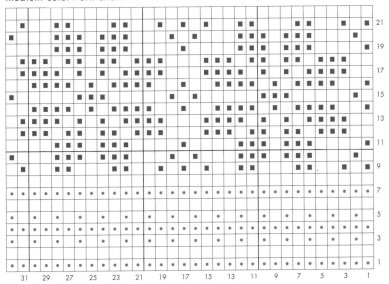

large colorwork chart

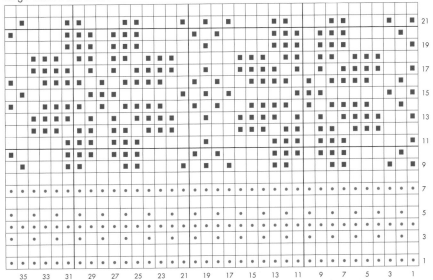

critter socks

....

This is another plain (and easy to knit) sock with a colorwork panel around the top of the leg. This pattern is designed and sized for children, with a choice of little cat faces or birds. You can use up small amounts of leftover yarn with these socks, as you need only a few yards for each of the contrast colors. They are a quick knit, so you can whip out a pair as an emergency gift in very little time.

SIZE Child's S (M, L), 5 (6, 7)" (12.5 [15, 18]cm) circumference, 6½" (16.5cm) long foot, and 8" (20.5cm) tall leg measured from the bottom of the foot to the top of the cuff

GAUGE 8 stitches and 12 rows = 1" (2.5cm) in stockinette stitch on US size 0 (2mm) needles using 1 color; 8 stitches and 10 rows = 1" (2.5cm) in stockinette stitch on US size 1 (2.5mm) needles in colorwork pattern

NEEDLES 2 US size 0 (2mm) and 2 US size 1 (2.5mm) circular needles (or 1 long circular needle each), or sizes needed to attain gauge

YARN Lorna's Laces Shepherd Sock, 80% superwash wool and 20% nylon, 2 oz (56.5g), 215 yd (196.5m), (**1**) Superfine

Cat Socks 1 (1, 2) skein(s) Whisper (color A), 20 yd (18.5m) Berry (color B), 20 yd (18.5m) Chocolate (color C)

Bird Socks 1 (1, 2) skeins Neptune (color A), 20 yd (18.5m) Caribbean (color B), 20 yd (18.5m) Citrus (color C)

TOE

With color A and the smaller needles, and using a Turkish Cast-On, a Figure-Eight Cast-On, or Judy's Magic Cast-On, cast on a total of 20 (24, 28) stitches—10 (12, 14) stitches on each needle. Knit across the stitches on each needle once. On the next round, increase 4 stitches as follows:
Needle 1 K1, m1, knit until the last stitch, m1, k1.

Needle 2 K1, m1, knit until the last stitch, m1, k1.
Then knit a round without increasing.
Repeat these 2 rounds until you have a total of 40 (48, 56) stitches—20 (24, 28) stitches on each needle.
Knit in stockinette stitch (knit every round) until approximately 2 (2¼, 2½)" (5 [5.5, 6.5]cm) shy of the total length of the sock.

CREATE THE GUSSET

Round 1 Knit across needle 1.
Needle 2 (sole stitches): K1, m1, knit across to the last stitch, m1, k1.
Round 2 Knit all stitches.
Repeat rounds 1 and 2 until there are 32 (40, 48) stitches total on needle 2. Work across needle 1.

TURN THE HEEL

You will now work back and forth on the stitches on needle 2 and will not work the stitches on needle 1 while turning the heel. Turn the heel as follows:

Row 1 K19 (23, 27), ssk, k1, turn.
Row 2 Sl1, p7, p2tog, p1, turn.
Row 3 Sl1, k8, ssk, k1, turn.
Row 4 Sl11, p9, p2tog, p1, turn.
Row 5 Sl1, k10, ssk, k1, turn.
Row 6 Sl1, p11, p2tog, p1, turn.

Continue in this manner until all of the stitches are worked and you have 20 (24, 28) stitches on the needle.

LEG

Begin working in the round again. On the right side, knit to the end of needle 2. Work across the instep stitches on needle 1.

Work in stockinette stitch until the sock measures 5" (12.5cm) from the bottom of the heel, or approximately 3" (7.5cm) shy of the desired leg length.

Start the Colorwork Pattern

Change to the larger-sized needles and work row 1 of the appropriate size of the Critter colorwork chart you are using, either the cat or the bird chart. You will work row 1 twice: once across needle 1 and once across needle 2.

Work all rows of the chart and then break off colors B and C.

Using color A, work in k1, p1 ribbing for 1" (2.5cm). Bind off loosely in rib.

BIRD CRITTER SOCKS

key

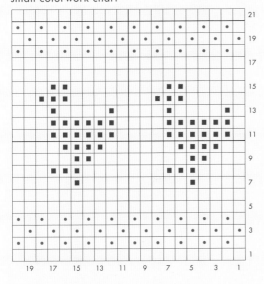

☐ Color A
• Color B
■ Color C

small colorwork chart

medium colorwork chart

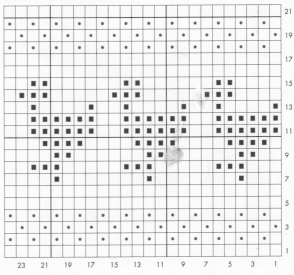

large colorwork chart

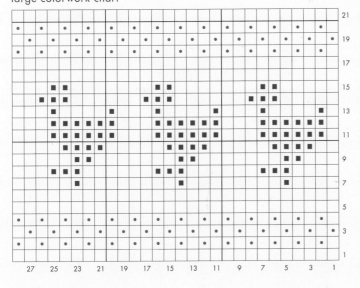

key

- Color A
- • Color B
- ■ Color C

small colorwork chart

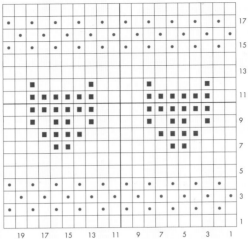

medium colorwork chart

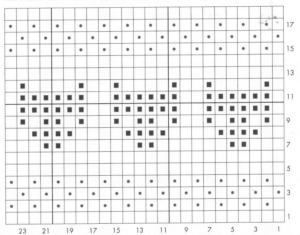

large colorwork chart

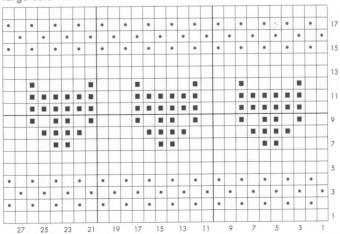

sanquhar socks

....

Sanquhar (pronounced "Sankhar") is a town in southern Scotland that became known in the eighteenth century as an important regional center for wool trading. The area also became known for distinctive two-color knitting, usually worked in black or navy and white or cream. Sanquhar knitting is most often used today in glove patterns, although I've seen hats and scarves knit in this style as well. Of course, I happen to think a pair of Sanquhar socks would make the most distinctive winter wear of all. The colors I chose are traditional, but the design would be equally striking using other high-contrast color combinations.

SIZE M (L), 8 (9)" (20.5 [23]cm) circumference, 9" (23cm) long foot, and 10" (25.5cm) tall leg measured from the bottom of the foot to the top of the cuff.

GAUGE 8 stitches and 12 rows = 1" (2.5cm) in stockinette stitch on US size 0 (2mm) needles using 1 color; 8 stitches and 10 rows = 1" (2.5cm) in stockinette stitch on US size 1 (2.5mm) needles in colorwork pattern

NEEDLES 2 US size 0 (2mm) and 2 US size 1 (2.5mm) circular needles, or sizes needed to attain gauge

YARN Cherry Tree Hill Supersock Solids, 100% luxury merino fingering weight, 4 oz (113.5g), 420 yd (384m), 1 skein Natural (color A), 1 skein Black (color B), (**1**) Superfine

TOE

With color A and the smaller needles, and using a Turkish Cast-On, a Figure-Eight Cast-On, or Judy's Magic Cast-On, cast on a total of 30 (34) stitches—15 (17) stitches on each needle. Knit across the stitches on each needle once. On the next round, increase 4 stitches as follows:

Needle 1 K1, m1, knit until the last stitch, m1, k1.

Needle 2 K1, m1, knit until the last stitch, m1, k1.

Then knit a round without increasing.

Repeat these 2 rounds until you have a total of 66 (74) stitches—33 (37) stitches on each needle.

START THE COLORWORK PATTERN

Change to the larger-sized needles: Needle 1 holds the instep stitches, and needle 2 holds the sole stitches. Work the first row of Sanquhar chart A over needle 1 and the first row of Sanquhar chart B over needle 2. Note that you will work the 2 stitches of chart B 16 (18) times and then end working the first stitch once, for a total of 33 (37) stitches.

Continue in this manner, working rows 1–20 of chart A and rows 1 and 2 of chart B in as many repeats as needed until the foot is approximately 3" (7.5cm) shy of the desired finished length.

CREATE THE GUSSET

Round 1 Work across needle 1 in the chart A pattern. Needle 2 (sole stitches): Keeping the stitches in the proper color sequence to follow chart B, k1, m1, knit across to the last stitch, m1, k1.

Round 2 Work across needle 1 in the chart A pattern. Needle 2 (sole stitches): Work across in the chart B pattern.

Repeat rounds 1 and 2 until you have 45 (49) stitches total on needle 2, incorporating the extra stitches in the chart B pattern. Work across needle 1 in pattern and break off color B.

You will leave the 33 (37) instep stitches on the needle (you will not work on these stitches while you turn the heel). Move the 45 (49) heel stitches onto one of the smaller-sized needles. Using color A only, work a short-row heel on the 45 (49) heel stitches as follows.

WORK THE SHORT-ROW HEEL

Row 1 Knit 38 (42) stitches. Move the working yarn as if to purl. Slip the next, unworked stitch from the left needle to the right needle. Turn your work.

Row 2 Slip this unworked stitch from the left needle to the right needle. Purl the next stitch (you will have wrapped that first stitch around its base with the working yarn), and purl across 31 (35) stitches. Move the working yarn as if to knit and slip the next stitch. Turn.

Row 3 Slip this unworked stitch and knit across to the last stitch before

the unworked wrapped stitch. Wrap and turn.

Row 4 Slip the first stitch and purl across to the stitch before the unworked wrapped stitch. Wrap and turn.

Repeat rows 3 and 4 until 11 (12) of the colorwork stitches are wrapped and on the left side, 11 (13) stitches are "live" in the middle, and 11 (12) are wrapped and on the right side. There will be 6 gusset stitches unwrapped and unworked at each end of the needle. At this stage, you should be ready to work a right-side row. Your heel turn is half done.

Note How many stitches you leave unworked in the middle depends on how wide you want your sock heel to be. If you want it a bit wider or narrower than the pattern specifies, do a couple fewer or more short rows, respectively. Two short rows equal about ¼" (6mm).

Now work the second half of the heel:

Row 1 Knit across the 11 (13) live stitches to the first unworked, wrapped stitch. To work this stitch, pick up the wrap and knit it together with the stitch.

Wrap the next stitch (so that it now has two wraps) and turn.

Row 2 Slip the first (double-wrapped) stitch and purl across to the first unworked, wrapped stitch. Pick up the wrap and purl it together with the stitch. Wrap the next stitch and turn.

On subsequent rows, you will pick up both wraps and knit or purl them together with the stitch.

Continue until you have worked all of the wrapped stitches, and work to the end of the row over the last 6 stitches.

Knit a mini heel flap

Work back and forth on the heel stitches on needle 2 as follows:

Row 1 (RS) K38 (42), ssk, turn.

Row 2 Sl1, p31 (35), p2tog, turn.

Row 3 [Sl1, k1] 16 (18) times, ssk, turn.

Work rows 2 and 3 until you have 33 (37) stitches remaining.

LEG

Begin working in the round again. Move the heel stitches back onto one of the larger needles.

You will now start working the chart A pattern on the stitches on needle 2, ensuring that you are starting in the right place on the chart so that it corresponds with the chart on needle 1. Work until the sock measures approximately 8" (20.5cm) tall from the bottom of the heel, or 2" (5cm) shy of the desired finished length, ending after having worked round 10 or 20 of the chart. Work a k1, p1 corrugated ribbing as follows:

Knit 1 in color B, purl 1 in color A around, for 24 rounds.

Break off color A and bind off loosely using color B only.

SANQUHAR SOCKS

key

☐ Color A
■ Color B

chart b

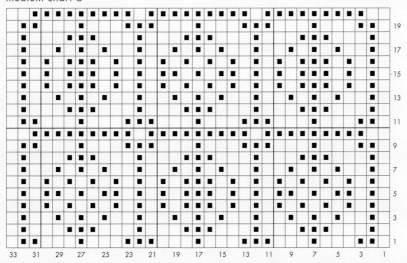

medium chart a

large chart a

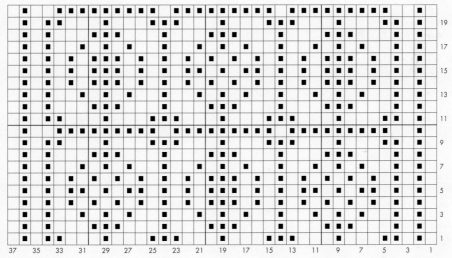

norwegian rose socks

· ·

I've long been a fan of traditional Norwegian colorwork and have knit my share of Norwegian sweaters, hats, and mittens. These socks are my salute to one of the most beautiful styles of colorwork I know. The rose is a familiar motif in traditional Norwegian knitting, and years ago I designed and started to knit a coat with a stylized rose as the central motif. The less said about that endeavor the better, and fortunately this sock has proved a much more manageable project. This pattern also exemplifies how striking nontraditional color combinations can be. I've chosen green and brown for this design not because it is often seen in Norwegian knits but simply because it reminds me of mint chocolate chip ice cream. As always when you knit, feel free to go a little wild with your own unique ideas and inspirations.

SIZE M (L), 8½" (9½") (21.5 [24]cm) circumference, 9" (23cm) long foot, and 12½" (32cm) tall leg measured from the bottom of the foot to the top of the cuff

GAUGE 8 stitches and 12 rows = 1" (2.5cm) in stockinette stitch on US size 0 (2mm) needles using 1 color; 8 stitches and 10 rows = 1" (2.5cm) in stockinette stitch on US size 1 (2.5mm) needles in colorwork pattern

NEEDLES 2 US size 0 (2mm) and 2 US size 1 (2.5mm) circular needles, or sizes needed to attain gauge

YARN Shibui Knits Sock, 100% superwash merino wool, 1¾ oz (50g), 191 yd (174.5m), 2 skeins Bark (color A), 2 skeins Kiwi (color B), **(1)** Superfine

TOE

With color A and the smaller needles, and using a Turkish Cast-On, a Figure-Eight Cast-On, or Judy's Magic Cast-On, cast on a total of 30 (34) stitches—15 (17) stitches on each needle. Knit across the stitches on each needle once.

On the next round, increase 4 stitches as follows:
Needle 1 K1, m1, knit until the last stitch, m1, k1.
Needle 2 K1, m1, knit until the last stitch, m1, k1.
Then knit a round without increasing.

Repeat these 2 rounds until you have a total of 66 (74) stitches—33 (37) stitches on each needle.

START THE COLORWORK PATTERN

Change to the larger-sized needles: Needle 1 holds the instep stitches, and needle 2 holds the sole stitches. Work the charts as follows:

On needle 1, work the first row of side chart A (4, 6 stitches), work the first row of the Norwegian Rose colorwork chart (25 stitches), and then work the first row of side chart B (4, 6 stitches). Work the first row of the sole chart over needle 2: Work the 4-stitch chart 8 (9) times, end after working stitch 1 of the chart.

Continue in this manner, working rows 1–26 of the Norwegian Rose chart, rows 1–3 of the side charts, and rows 1 and 2 of the sole chart in as many repeats as needed until the foot is approximately 3" (7.5cm) shy of the desired finished length.

CREATE THE GUSSET

Round 1 Work across needle 1 in pattern. Needle 2 (sole stitches): Keeping the stitches in the proper color sequence to follow the sole chart, k1, m1, knit across to the last stitch, m1, k1.

Round 2 Work across needle 1 in pattern. Needle 2 (sole stitches): Work across in the sole chart pattern.

Repeat rounds 1 and 2 until you have 45 (49) stitches total on needle 2, incorporating the extra stitches in the sole chart pattern. Work across needle 1 in pattern and break off color B.

You will leave the 33 (37) instep stitches on the needle (you will not work on these stitches while you turn the heel). Move the 45 (49) heel stitches onto one of the smaller-sized needles. Using color A

only, work a short-row heel on the 45 (49) heel stitches as follows.

WORK THE SHORT-ROW HEEL

Row 1 Knit 38 (42) stitches. Move the working yarn as if to purl. Slip the next, unworked stitch from the left needle to the right needle. Turn your work.

Row 2 Slip this unworked stitch from the left needle to the right needle. Purl the next stitch (you will have wrapped that first stitch around its base with the working yarn) and purl across 31 (35) stitches. Move the working yarn as if to knit and slip the next stitch. Turn.

Row 3 Slip this unworked stitch and knit across to the last stitch before the unworked wrapped stitch. Wrap and turn.

Row 4 Slip the first stitch and purl across to the stitch before the unworked wrapped stitch. Wrap and turn.

Repeat rows 3 and 4 until 11 (12) of the colorwork stitches are wrapped and on the left side, 11 (13) stitches are "live" in the middle, and 11 (12) are wrapped and on the right side. There will be 6 gusset stitches unwrapped and unworked at each end of the needle. At this stage, you should be ready to work a right-side row. Your heel turn is half done.

Note How many stitches you leave unworked in the middle depends on how wide you want your sock heel to be. If you want it a bit wider than the pattern specifies, do a couple fewer short rows. If you want it a bit narrower, do a couple more short

rows. Two short rows equal about ¼" (6mm).

Now you'll work the second half of the heel:

Row 1 Knit across the 11 (13) live stitches across to the first unworked, wrapped stitch. To work this stitch, pick up the wrap and knit it together with the stitch.

Wrap the next stitch (so that it now has two wraps) and turn.

Row 2 Slip the first (double-wrapped) stitch and purl across to the first unworked, wrapped stitch. Pick up the wrap and purl it together with the stitch. Wrap the next stitch and turn.

On subsequent rows, you will pick up both wraps and knit or purl them together with the stitch. Continue until you have worked all of the wrapped stitches, and work to the end of the row over the last 6 stitches.

Knit a mini heel flap

Work back and forth on the heel stitches on needle 2 as follows:

Row 1 (RS) K38 (42), ssk, turn.

Row 2 Sl1, p31 (35), p2tog, turn.

Row 3 [Sl1, k1] 16 (18) times, ssk, turn.

Work rows 2 and 3 until you have 33 (37) stitches remaining.

LEG

Begin working in the round again. Move the heel stitches back onto one of the larger needles.

You will now start working the side charts and the Norwegian Rose chart patterns on the stitches on needle 2, ensuring that you are starting in the right place on the chart so that it corresponds with the chart on needle 1. Work until the sock measures approximately 10½" (26.5cm) from the bottom of the heel, or 2" (5cm) shy of the desired finished length, ending after having worked round 26 of the Norwegian Rose chart.

Work a k1, p1 corrugated ribbing as follows:

Knit 1 in color B, purl 1 in color A around, for 12 rounds.

Break off color A and bind off loosely in color B.

NORWEGIAN ROSE SOCKS

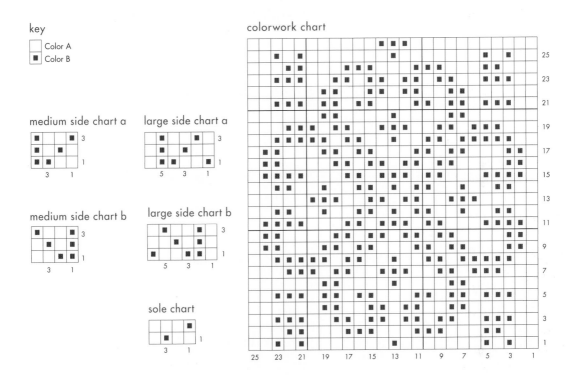

key

☐ Color A
■ Color B

colorwork chart

medium side chart a

large side chart a

medium side chart b

large side chart b

sole chart

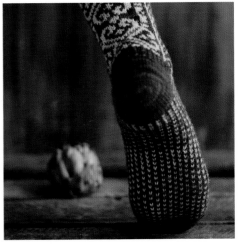

fair isle socks

....

Fair Isle knitting, named after Fair Isle in Scotland, where it originated, uses relatively small repeating motifs in bands, and never more than two colors per row, although a garment may be made up of many different colors overall. I could have called these socks "Cheater's Fair Isle Socks" because I've created the illusion of multiple colors by using a variegated yarn for the foreground and a solid color yarn for the background color. You could also pair a self-striping yarn with a solid for another multicolor look. These combinations are a great way to make your socks look difficult and time-consuming while keeping the actual knitting as simple as possible.

SIZE M, 8" (20.5cm) circumference, 9" (23cm) long foot, and 9" (23cm) tall leg measured from the bottom of the foot to the top of the cuff

GAUGE 8½ stitches and 12 rows = 1" (2.5cm) in stockinette stitch worked in 2 colors on US size 1 (2.5mm) needles in colorwork pattern

NEEDLES 2 US size 1 (2.5mm) circular needles, or size needed to attain gauge

YARN Shibui Knits Sock, 100% superwash merino wool, 1¾ oz (50g), 191 yd (174.5m), 2 skeins Ivory (color A), 1 skein Jewel (color B), **①** Superfine

NOTE Please be sure to check your gauge and adjust your needle size accordingly. Although this pattern is offered in one size only because of the limitations of the pattern motif, you can make some adjustments in the size of the finished sock by going up or down a needle size.

TOE
With color A and using a Turkish Cast-On, a Figure-Eight Cast-On, or Judy's Magic Cast-On, cast on a total of 32 stitches—16 stitches on each needle. Knit across the stitches on each needle once. On the next round, increase 4 stitches as follows:

Needle 1 K1, m1, knit until the last stitch, m1, k1.
Needle 2 K1, m1, knit until the last stitch, m1, k1.
Then knit a round without increasing.
Repeat these 2 rounds until you have a total of 72 stitches—36 stitches on each needle. On the

last round 2, increase 1 stitch in the middle of needle 2 for a total of 37 stitches on needle 2.

START THE COLORWORK PATTERN
Needle 1 holds the instep stitches, and needle 2 holds the sole stitches. Work the first row of the 12 stitches of the Fair Isle chart 3 times over

needle 1 and the first row of the 4 stitches of the sole chart 9 times over needle 2; then work stitch 1 again.

Continue in this manner, working rows 1–26 of the Fair Isle colorwork chart and rows 1 and 2 of the sole chart in as many repeats as needed until approximately 2½" (6.5cm) shy of the desired finished length.

CREATE THE GUSSET

Round 1 Work across needle 1 in the Fair Isle chart pattern. Needle 2 (sole stitches): Keeping the stitches in the proper color sequence to follow the sole chart, k1, m1, knit across to the last stitch, m1, k1.

Round 2 Work across needle 1 in the Fair Isle chart pattern. Needle 2 (sole stitches): Work across in the sole chart pattern.

Repeat rounds 1 and 2 until you have 49 stitches total on needle 2. Work across needle 1 in pattern and break off color B.

You will leave the 36 instep stitches on the needle (you will not work on these stitches while you turn the heel). Using color A only, work a short-row heel on the 49 heel stitches as follows.

WORK THE SHORT-ROW HEEL

Row 1 Knit 42 stitches. Move the working yarn as if to purl. Slip the next, unworked stitch from the left needle to the right needle. Turn your work.

Row 2 Slip this unworked stitch from the left needle to the right needle. Purl the next stitch (you will have wrapped that first stitch around its base with the working

yarn), and purl across 35 stitches. Move the working yarn as if to knit and slip the next stitch. Turn.

Row 3 Slip this unworked stitch and knit across to the last stitch before the unworked wrapped stitch. Wrap and turn.

Row 4 Slip the first stitch and purl across to the stitch before the unworked wrapped stitch. Wrap and turn.

Repeat rows 3 and 4 until 12 of the colorwork stitches are wrapped and on the left side, 13 stitches are "live" in the middle, and 12 are wrapped and on the right. There will be 6 gusset stitches unwrapped and unworked at each end of the needle. At this stage, you should be

ready to work a right-side row. Your heel turn is half done.

Note How many stitches you leave unworked in the middle depends on how wide you want your sock heel to be. If you want it a bit wider than the pattern specifies, do a couple fewer short rows. If you want it a bit narrower, do a couple more short rows. Two short rows equal about ¼" (6mm).

Now work the second half of the heel:

Row 1 Knit across the 13 live stitches to the first unworked, wrapped stitch. To work this stitch, pick up the wrap and knit it together with the stitch.

· ·

FAIR ISLE SOCKS

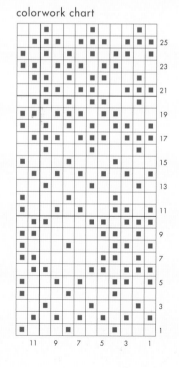

key

☐ Color A
■ Color B

sole chart

colorwork chart

· ·

Wrap the next stitch (so that it now has two wraps) and turn.

Row 2 Slip the first (double-wrapped) stitch and purl across to the first unworked, wrapped stitch. Pick up the wrap and purl it together with the stitch. Wrap the next stitch and turn.

On subsequent rows, you will pick up both wraps and knit or purl them together with the stitch. Continue until you have worked all of the wrapped stitches, and work to the end of the row over the last 6 stitches.

Knit a mini heel flap

Work back and forth on the heel stitches on needle 2 as follows:

Row 1 (RS) K42, ssk, turn.
Row 2 Sl1, p35, p2tog, turn.
Row 3 [Sl1, k1] 18 times, ssk, turn.

Work rows 2 and 3 until you have 37 stitches remaining. Purl across these stitches, decreasing one in the center of the round so that you now have 36 stitches on needle 2.

LEG

Begin working in the round again. You will now start working the Fair Isle chart pattern on the stitches on needle 2, ensuring that you are starting in the right place on the chart so that it corresponds with the chart on needle 1.

Work until your sock measures approximately 7" (18cm) from the bottom of the heel, or 2" (5cm) shy of the desired leg length, ending after completing row 3 or 15 of the chart. Break off color B and using color A only, work in k2, p2 ribbing for 2" (5cm). Bind off loosely in rib.

hot stuff! socks

....

*My brother Dave is a car guy and loves 1970s muscle cars. Although he
has never owned a car with flames painted down the side, whenever I see
one I think of Dave, and so I worked up this design with him in mind. These
socks are great fun if you use a solid or semisolid color for the background
and a variegated handpaint for the flames, as I have done here. While the
charts for this design are pretty complex, don't let that scare you. If you
are off by a stitch here or there, no one will ever know. And if it really
bothers you, there is always duplicate stitch to the rescue (page 94)!*

SIZE M (L), 8 (9)" (20.5 [23]cm)
circumference, 9" (23cm) long foot, and
10" (25.5cm) tall leg measured from the
bottom of the foot to the top of the cuff

GAUGE 8 stitches and 12 rows = 1"
(2.5cm) in stockinette stitch on US size 0
(2mm) needles using 1 color; 8 stitches
and 10 rows = 1" (2.5cm) in stockinette
stitch on US size 1 (2.5mm) needles in
colorwork pattern

NEEDLES 2 US size 0 (2mm) and 2 US
size 1 (2.5mm) circular needles (or 1 long
circular needle each), or sizes needed to
attain gauge

YARN Socks That Rock Lightweight, 100%
superwash merino wool, 4½ oz (127.5g),
360 yd (329m), 1 skein Shadow (color A),
1 skein Firebird (color B), **1** Superfine

TOE

With color A and the smaller
needles, and using a Turkish
Cast-On, a Figure-Eight Cast-On,
or Judy's Magic Cast-On, cast on
a total of 30 (34) stitches—15 (17)
stitches on each needle. Knit across
the stitches on each needle once.
On the next round, increase 4
stitches as follows:
Needle 1 K1, m1, knit until the last
stitch, m1, k1.

Needle 2 K1, m1, knit until the last
stitch, m1, k1.
Then knit a round without
increasing.
Repeat these 2 rounds until you
have a total of 66 (74) stitches—33
(37) stitches on each needle.
Knit in stockinette stitch (knit every
round) until approximately 3"
(7.5cm) shy of the total length of
the foot.

CREATE THE GUSSET

Round 1 Knit across needle 1.
Needle 2 (sole stitches): K1, m1,
knit across to the last stitch, m1, k1.
Round 2 Knit all stitches.
Repeat rounds 1 and 2 until you
have 55 (61) stitches total on needle
2. Work across needle 1.

TURN THE HEEL

You will work back and forth on the stitches on needle 2 and will not knit the stitches on needle 1 while turning the heel. Turn the heel as follows:

Row 1 (RS) K37 (41), kf&b, k1, w&t.

Row 2 P22 (24), pf&b, p1, w&t.

Row 3 K20 (22), kf&b, k1, w&t.

Row 4 P18 (20), pf&b, p1, w&t.

Row 5 K16 (18), kf&b, k1, w&t.

Row 6 P14 (16), pf&b, p1, w&t.

Row 7 K12 (14), kf&b, k1, w&t.

Row 8 P10 (12), pf&b, p1, w&t.

Needle 2 now holds 63 (69) stitches, having just completed a wrong-side row. On the right side, knit to the end of needle 2, knitting each wrap together with the stitch it wraps. Work across the instep stitches on needle 1.

HEEL FLAP

Work back and forth on the stitches on needle 2:

HOT STUFF! SOCKS

key

☐ Color A
■ Color B

medium chart a

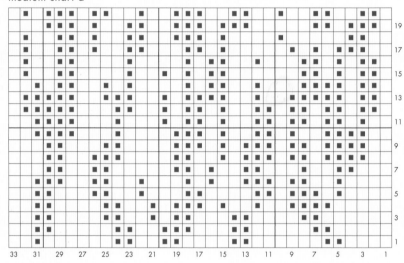

medium chart b

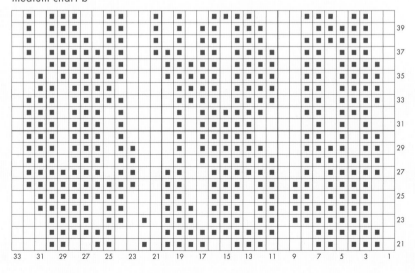

Row 1 (RS) K47 (52) (knitting each wrap together with the stitch it wraps), ssk, turn.

Row 2 Sl1, p31 (35), p2tog, turn.

Row 3 [Sl1, k1] 16 (18) times, ssk, turn.

Repeat rows 2 and 3 until all side stitches have been worked; end having worked row 2.

LEG

Begin working in the round again.

Start the Colorwork Pattern

Change to the larger-sized needles and work row 1 of Hot Stuff! chart A. You will work row 1 twice: once across needle 1 and once across needle 2. Work all 20 rounds of Hot Stuff! chart A; then work Hot Stuff! chart B (rounds 21–40) and Hot Stuff! chart C (rounds 41–61) in the same manner.

Break off color B. Knit 1 round in color A. Work in k1, p1 ribbing for 1" (2.5cm) using color A only. Bind off loosely in rib.

medium chart c

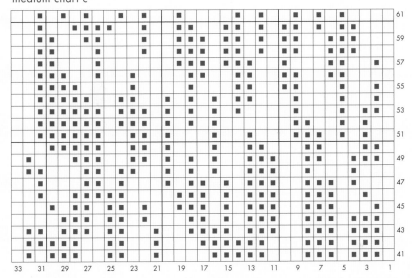

large chart a

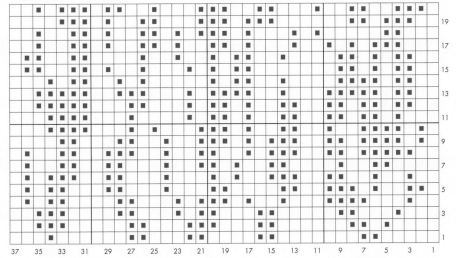

HOT STUFF! SOCKS (CONT.)

key

☐ Color A
■ Color B

large chart b

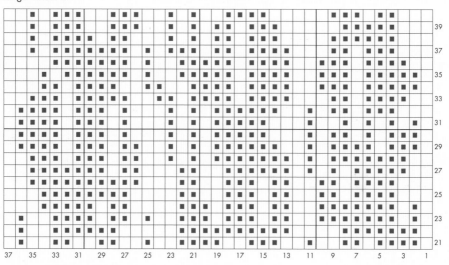

large chart c

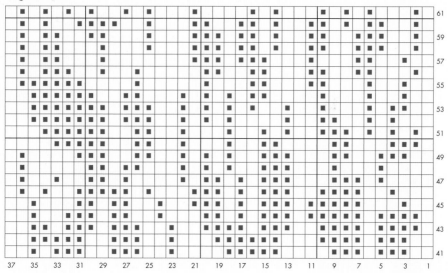

appendix

·······································

techniques for toe-up socks

This section includes techniques you need to know to knit socks from the toe up. If you are a veteran toe-up knitter, you might find this section useful as a refresher course. If you are new to the toe-up way of sock knitting, everything you need to know to get started is right here.

The different needle techniques you can use to knit socks in the round are demonstrated here. If you are not new to knitting socks, you probably already have a preferred technique, but if you were taught one way and are interested in trying something different, have a look. I've also included instructions for four great cast-ons, which can be used interchangeably for any of my patterns. You can try a couple of different cast-ons to find the one that suits you best. The three different heels that I use in my patterns are also shown. In many cases, it is possible to switch out one heel technique for another in the sock patterns if you have a strong preference for one over another. Really, the only restrictions on switching out heels in these patterns are in the colorwork socks (discussed in greater detail on page 92), so feel free to experiment. I've also included two easy bind-offs that are nicely stretchy and perfect for finishing off the cuffs of your socks.

NEEDLE TECHNIQUES

There are three ways to knit socks in the round: on double-pointed needles, on two circular needles, or on one circular needle employing what is called the Magic Loop technique.

knitting a sock on double-pointed needles   When I knit socks on double-pointed needles, I prefer needles no shorter than 5" (12.75 cm) and no longer than 7" (17.75 cm). Any shorter and I won't have room for all the stitches on the needles, unless I am making children's socks. Any longer, and I spend too much valuable knitting time pushing my stitches to the business end of the needle. I also find that long double-points stab me in the palm of the hand when I'm knitting small circumference projects.

To knit socks on a set of five double-pointed needles, you divide your stitches over four of the needles and use the fifth needle to knit the stitches off one needle to another.

After creating your toe, divide your stitches over four of the five needles. **(a)**

Pick up your work so that the start of your round is on the first needle in your left hand and the end of the round is on the last needle in your right hand.

Using the fifth double-pointed needle (the one that you did not put any stitches on), work the first stitch on the left needle as desired. Pull the yarn tight to avoid a hole. **(b)** Continue to work the stitches on the left needle. When all of the stitches have been worked off the left needle, that one will become the free needle.

Now use the newly free needle to work the stitches on the next needle. Continue working until you come to the end of the round.

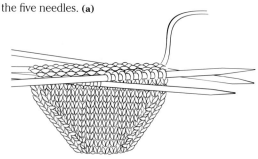

(a) double-pointed needles

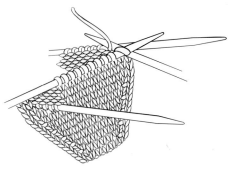

(b) double-pointed needles

knitting a sock on two circular needles

To knit a sock on two circulars, I like to use needles that are 16" (40 cm) to 24" (60 cm) in length. Any longer and I find that the dangling end of the needle not in use gets in my way. Some people like to use needles of two different lengths (for example, one 16" [40cm] needle and one 24" [60cm] needle) so they can easily tell them apart and more quickly grab the correct needle to knit.

Begin by dividing your toe stitches over the two needles: instep stitches on one needle, and sole/heel stitches on the other. **(c)**

With your work facing you, slide the stitches to the right-hand point of the needle. Start knitting by working these with the needle point that is on the other end of that same circular needle. **(d)**

Knit until you have worked all of the stitches on the first circular needle. Slide the worked stitches down onto the needle's cable and turn the work so the other needle is in front.

Now work the stitches on the second needle. Slide the stitches to the right-hand point of the needle so that the first stitch is at the working end of the needle. Knit the first stitch firmly to tighten up any gap between the two needles.

knitting a sock on one long circular needle (the magic loop technique)

To use the Magic Loop technique, you want a relatively long circular needle—at least 32" (80 cm) long. I find this technique easiest when working with a needle that is at least 40" (100 cm) long. The longer needle allows for plenty of room to manipulate the cable as needed.

Divide the toe stitches so that half are on one needle tip and half are on the other needle tip. The stitches you are going to start knitting are on the front needle, and the needle cable is looped on the left side of the work as you are facing it. **(e)**

Pull the back needle tip out to the right so that the stitches slide onto the cable. Pull it out far enough so that you can easily use the back needle tip to knit the front stitches. You now have a loop of cable on each side of your work. **(f)**

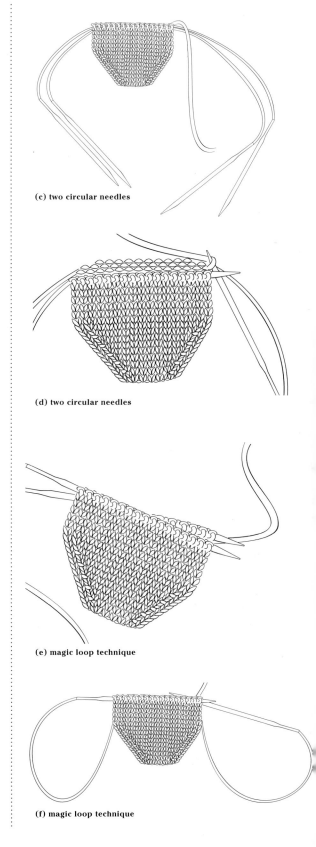

(c) two circular needles

(d) two circular needles

(e) magic loop technique

(f) magic loop technique

When you have worked all of stitches on the front needle (half the round has been completed), turn the work around and return the stitches to the position shown in illustration **(e)**. The stitches you're about to knit are in front (closest to you), and the working yarn is on the right side of the needle in back.

CAST-ONS

All of these techniques are invisible cast-ons that create a closed end, so they are perfect for starting a sock toe.

figure-eight cast-on   This cast-on can be a little fiddly at the start, but it's an easy technique to memorize, so you can do it "on the go" without having instructions in front of you every time. You will need two circular needles. They can be different lengths but should be the same needle size.

Hold the two circular needles with the points parallel. Hold the tail of the yarn against the front of the bottom needle; then bring the yarn from the front to the back between the needles, and wrap it up and over from behind the top needle, then down in front of the top needle and between the needles again, from front to back, and around the bottom needle. You are wrapping your yarn around the needles in a figure eight. **(a)**

If your goal is to have, for example, a total of 16 stitches, you want to have 8 loops on each needle, as shown. **(b)**

The working yarn is going between the needles from front to back, and the last loop is over the bottom needle. Turn your work upside down so that what was the bottom needle is now on the top. Pull what is now the bottom needle out carefully so that the bottom stitches dangle on the cable of the needle.

Using the free end of the top circular needle, knit the 8 stitches on that needle. **(c)**

Now turn the work again so that the bottom needle with the unworked loops is now on top. Making sure to hold your working yarn tight, and using the other end of the top circular needle, knit the 8 stitches on the top needle. For this initial row, the stitches will be twisted the wrong way, so you will need to knit into the backs of the loops when you encounter these twisted stitches. **(d)**

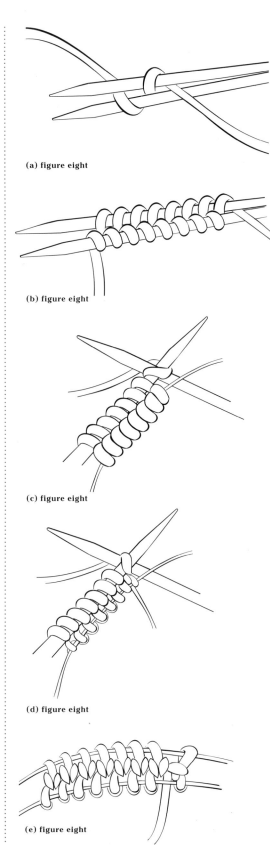

(a) figure eight

(b) figure eight

(c) figure eight

(d) figure eight

(e) figure eight

Work 2 more rows like this so that you have completed 4 rows. You will have a needle at the top of your work with 8 stitches on it and a needle at the bottom of your work with 8 stitches on it. **(e)**

You have completed the "set-up" for your toe. The stitches in the middle of your work may be loose, but you can tighten them up a little by working the excess yarn toward one side after you have completed a couple of rounds.

Start the increases. Work the first round as follows:

Needle 1 K1, m1, knit to the last stitch, m1, k1.

Needle 2 K1, m1, knit to the last stitch, m1, k1.

Knit 1 round without increasing. **(f)**

Repeat these 2 rounds until you have the total number of stitches you need for your sock, half on needle 1 and half on needle 2. **(g)**

turkish cast-on The Turkish Cast-On is very similar to the Figure-Eight Cast-On, but at the start, when you wrap the yarn around the two needles, instead of alternating between needles in the figure-eight pattern you wrap the yarn around both needles at the same time.

For the Turkish Cast-On, you need two circular needles of the same size. They can be different lengths.

Make a slip knot on the top needle.

Hold the needles in your right hand with the points together, facing left, and wrap the working yarn around both needles, working left to right, half the number of times that you want the total number of stitches to be. **(h)** For example, do 8 wraps for a total of 16 stitches. (Do not count the slip knot on the top needle.) **(i)**

Turn your work upside down so that what was the bottom needle is now on the top, and pull the bottom needle out until the wrapped loops are sitting in the middle of the cable of the needle; allow this needle to dangle. Bring the non-working end of the top needle up to knit into the loops on the top needle. **(j)**

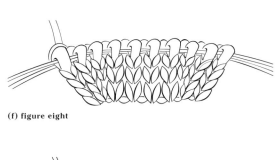

(f) figure eight

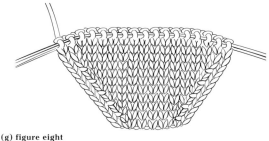

(g) figure eight

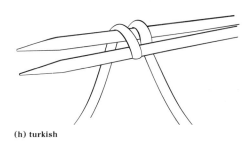

(h) turkish

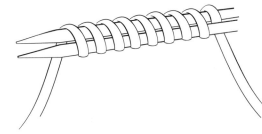

(i) turkish

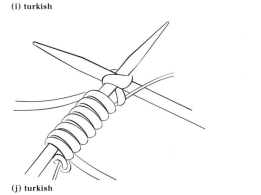

(j) turkish

After knitting the loops on the top needle, turn your work upside down. Slide the loops on the cable of what is now the top needle onto the tip of that needle, and slide the stitches just worked on the cable of the now bottom needle.

At this point, slide the slip knot off the tip of the needle and undo it, allowing it to hang. **(k)**

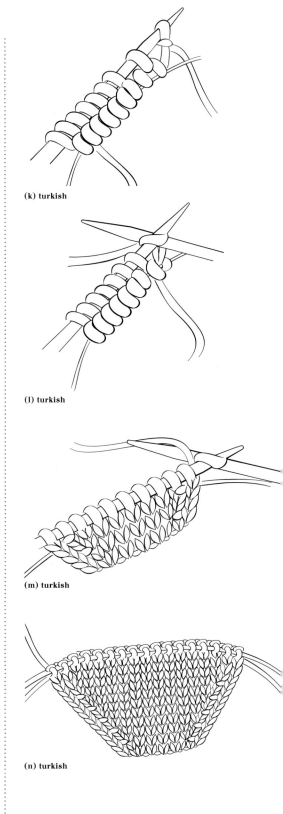

(k) turkish

With the working yarn, which is coming from the last stitch on the other needle, knit across the loops with this needle. Be sure to pull the yarn snug as you work the first stitch to avoid a gap. **(l)**

Pull the needle through to the right so that the stitches just worked are on the cable and the needle is dangling. Turn. Slide the stitches to the tip of the now top needle, and knit across the stitches with the other end of this needle.

(l) turkish

After 2 rounds worked in this manner, start the increases. Work the first round as follows:

Needle 1 K1, m1, knit until the last stitch, m1, k1.

Needle 2 K1, m1, knit until the last stitch, m1, k1.

Then knit 1 round without increasing. **(m)**

(m) turkish

Repeat these 2 rounds until you have the total number of stitches you need for your sock, half on needle 1 and half on needle 2. **(n)**

(n) turkish

judy's magic cast-on Judy's Magic Cast-On is my favorite cast-on method for toe-up socks. Once you get the hang of this technique, it is quick and easy to execute and makes a perfect toe every time. Its creator, Judy Becker, has once again given me permission to document this technique here.

I find that the easiest way to work this cast-on is with two circular needles, but if you are a die-hard user of double-pointed needles, you can find instructions for the cast-on using double-pointed needles on Judy's website (www.persistentillusion.com).

You will need two circular needles of the same size. They can be different lengths.

Hold the two needles together in your right hand, one on top of the other. Pull out some yarn from your skein. How much you pull out depends on how many stitches you are casting on. For a total of 16 stitches (8 on the top needle and 8 on the bottom needle), pull out about a 12" (30.5cm) tail of yarn.

Loop the yarn around the top needle so that the working yarn (the strand attached to the skein) is coming up from the bottom and the tail is in the back. **(o)**

With your left hand, pick up the yarn so that the tail goes over your index finger and the working yarn goes over your thumb. Grasp both strands of yarn with the rest of your fingers to hold the yarn in place on the needle. This will make a loop around the top needle that counts as 1 stitch. **(p)**

While holding the bottom strand firmly with your thumb, use your index finger to loop the yarn tail around the lower needle and pull it snug. You now have a loop (a stitch) on each needle. **(q)**

Now, while holding the yarn tail firmly with your index finger, bring the working yarn up with your thumb to loop around the top needle. There are now 2 stitches on the top needle: the loop you just cast on plus the first loop. **(r)**

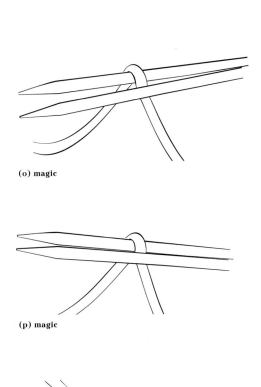

(o) magic

(p) magic

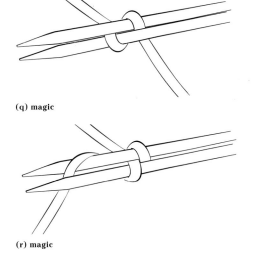

(q) magic

(r) magic

You will continue in this manner, casting on loops by alternating between the index finger and the thumb. The yarn tail controlled by your index finger always wraps around the bottom needle, and the working yarn strand controlled by your thumb always wraps around the top needle. Repeat these steps until you have cast on 8 stitches (or your desired number of stitches) onto each needle—a total of 16 stitches. **(s)**

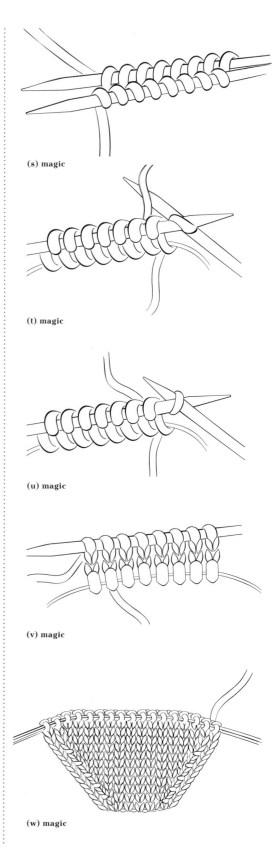

(s) magic

Now you are ready to begin knitting on these stitches. Turn the needles so that the bottom needle is now on the top. Pull the now bottom needle out until the stitches are sitting in the middle of the cable, and allow this needle to dangle. Pick up the working yarn. Make sure that the yarn tail is situated between the working yarn and the needle; otherwise, your first stitch will unravel.

While holding the yarn tail snug with your left hand, knit the row of stitches. If the first stitch becomes loose while you are knitting it, you can pull on the yarn tail to tighten it up. **(t)**

(t) magic

Turn the work so that the working yarn is on the right and the needle with the unworked stitches is now on the top. Pull the now bottom needle to the right so that the stitches you just knit are resting in the middle of the cable and allow this needle to dangle. Pull the top needle to the left so that its stitches are ready to knit, and knit these stitches. Note that these stitches will be twisted so that on this first round only you have to knit them through the back loops to reorient them so that they are sitting normally on the needle for the next round. **(u)** You have worked 1 complete round. **(v)**

(u) magic

You might find that the stitches are slightly uneven and loose. Remember to cast on over the needles at your usual cast-on gauge. Practice will make perfect—it may take you a few tries to get the hang of the perfect gauge.

(v) magic

You are now ready to work your increases. Work the first round as follows:

Needle 1 K1, m1, knit until the last stitch, m1, k1.

Needle 2 K1, m1, knit until the last stitch, m1, k1.

Then knit 1 round without increasing.

Repeat these 2 rounds until you have the total number of stitches you need for your sock, half on needle 1 and half on needle 2. **(w)**

(w) magic

short-row toe If you find the previous cast-ons a bit too fiddly for you, try the Short-Row Toe. This method starts with a provisional cast-on and knitting back and forth instead of immediately jumping into knitting in the round. The Short-Row Toe can be done using any needle technique you like: double-pointed needles, two circular needles, or the Magic Loop technique.

This demonstration is based on a sock that is 48 stitches around. It is started by provisionally casting on half of the total sock stitches—in this case, 24.

Using scrap yarn in a color that is different from the sock yarn being used, crochet a chain that is several chain stitches longer than the number of knit stitches you need. Use a smooth nonfuzzy yarn for the chain—picking up stitches in a chain crocheted from mohair or boucle is not easy! For a 24-stitch cast-on, I usually make my chain about 30 stitches long. Fasten off the last stitch and cut the yarn. Tie a knot in this tail of yarn—you are going to "unzip" this provisional cast-on later by undoing and pulling on this end, so the knot will make the correct end easier to find.

Look at the chain. One side of it (top) will be smooth and look like a row of little "v"s. The other side (bottom) will have a bump in the center of each vee.

Using your sock yarn and two double-pointed needles (or one circular needle), knit 1 stitch into the bump in the center of each little "v" on the bottom side of the chain until you have 24 stitches. **(x)**

Purl back across the stitches. You are ready to start the short rows.

Row 1 Knit 23 stitches. Move the working yarn as if to purl and slip the last stitch from the left needle to the right needle. Turn your work. **(y)**

Row 2 Slip the first, unworked stitch from the left needle to the right needle. Purl the next stitch (you will have wrapped that first stitch around its base with the working yarn), and purl across the next 21 stitches in the row. Move the working yarn as if to knit and slip the last stitch. Turn.

Row 3 Slip the first stitch and knit across to the last stitch before the unworked stitch. Wrap and turn.

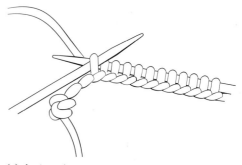

(x) short-row toe

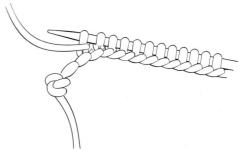

(y) short-row toe

Row 4 Slip the first stitch and purl across to the stitch before the unworked stitch. Wrap and turn. Continue working rows 3 and 4 in this manner. **(z)**

Work until 8 of the toe stitches are wrapped and on the left side, 8 stitches are "live" in the middle, and 8 are wrapped and on the right side. At this stage, you should be ready to work a right-side row. Your toe is half done.

Note How many stitches you leave unworked in the middle depends on how wide you want your sock toe to be. If you want it a bit wider than the pattern specifies, do a couple fewer short rows. If you want it a bit narrower, do a couple more short rows.

Now work the second half of the toe:

Row 1 Knit across the live stitches to the first unworked, wrapped stitch. On the next stitch, pick up the wrap and knit it together with the wrapped stitch.

Note The wrap sits almost horizontal around the vertical stitch. Put your needle through the horizontal wrap, then through the vertical stitch, and then knit the two together. **(aa)**

Wrap the next stitch (so that it now has two wraps) and turn. **(bb)**

Row 2 Slip the first (double-wrapped) stitch and purl across to the first unworked, wrapped stitch. Pick up the wrap and purl it together with the wrapped stitch. Wrap the next stitch and turn. **(cc)** On subsequent rows, you will pick up both wraps and knit or purl them together with the stitch.

Continue until you have worked all of the stitches and you once again have 24 live stitches. (If you are using double-pointed needles, divide the 24 stitches over 2 needles.)

Undo the cast-off end of your crocheted chain. Stick the point of a third double-pointed needle (or a second circular needle) into the stitch below the chain. Unzip the chain (like opening a bag of sugar), one stitch at a time, as you stick the tip of the needle into each stitch, moving each stitch onto the needle. **(dd)**

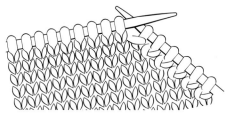

(z) short-row toe

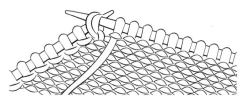

(aa) short-row toe

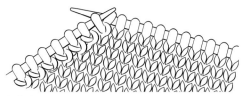

(bb) short-row toe

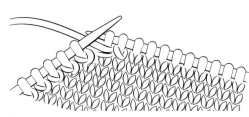

(cc) short-row toe

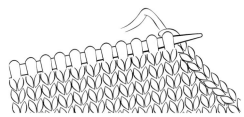

(dd) short-row toe

These stitches go on your second circular needle. If you are using double-pointed needles, divide these 24 stitches over the third and fourth needles. **(ee)**

On your first round after toe shaping, you may want to pick up an extra stitch or two between the live stitches and the stitches you've picked up from the cast-on, to close up any holes that might be there. On the next round, remember to decrease back down to the previous number of stitches per needle. You will now continue knitting the foot of your sock.

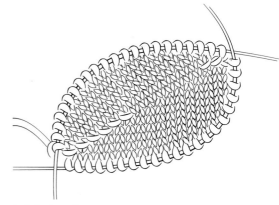

(ee) short-row toe

HEELS

All of the patterns in this book use one of the three heels described here: the gusset heel, the slip stitch heel, or the short-row heel with mini gusset. They are all fairly simple to work, and they mimic the look of a top-down heel.

gusset heel   The gusset heel is smooth and easy to do. I've used this heel for the children's sock patterns because in smaller sizes it doesn't add the unnecessary bulk that comes with the slip stitch heel.

You first create a gusset by increasing on every other round once you reach a certain point on the foot, where the "height" of the foot starts to increase as it connects to the ankle. After you have completed the increases specified in the pattern, you turn the heel by working short rows. You decrease 1 stitch at the end of each short row until you have decreased back down to your original stitch count.

slip stitch heel   The slip stitch heel starts out being worked like the gusset heel. Create the gusset by increasing on every other round once you reach a certain point on the foot, approximately 3" (7.5cm) shy of the desired total length of the foot. After you have completed the increases, you work on the heel stitches only, knitting some short rows to form the curve of the back of the heel. Then you knit the heel flap by working short rows, slipping alternate stitches and decreasing 1 stitch at the end of each short row until you have decreased back down to your original stitch count. I like this heel because it looks exactly like a traditional slip stitch heel sock that is worked from the top down.

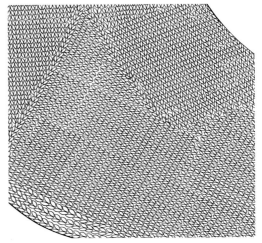

gusset heel

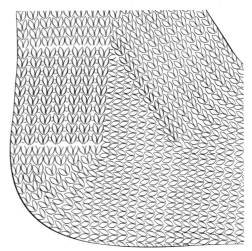

slip stitch heel

short-row heel with mini gusset The short-row heel is, to my eye, the one that looks most like a commercially produced sock. The variation of the short-row heel I use here combines a "regular" short-row heel with a small gusset for extra ease. I like to use this heel for colorwork socks because it involves no working across of the instep stitches (which are done in colorwork) once you start turning the heel.

You start by working gusset increases as you would for the other heel types, but with fewer increases. Then the short-row heel is knit like the short-row toe except that instead of starting with a crocheted chain and working a provisional cast-on, you already have live stitches. After working the heel portion, you work a mini heel flap in the same manner as the slip stitch heel, working across short rows, slipping alternate stitches, and decreasing 1 stitch at the end of each short row until you have decreased back down to your original stitch count.

After you have completed the heel, you resume knitting in the round on all stitches.

BIND-OFFS

The bind-off is a crucial element for a toe-up sock: If your bind-off is too tight, you won't be able to get the sock on a foot. The two bind-offs demonstrated here are nicely stretchy and perfect for finishing off your sock cuffs.

sewn bind-off The sewn bind-off is quick and easy to do, making it one of my favorites. When you work it, be sure not to pull the yarn too tight through the stitches. You want the edge to be nice and stretchy. What might look somewhat ruffled and unattractive with the sock off the leg looks smooth while the sock is being worn.

When you have finished knitting the cuff of your sock, cut the yarn, leaving a tail at least 18" (45.5cm) long. Thread the tail through a tapestry needle. First, insert the yarn through the first 2 stitches on the needle as if to purl, and gently pull all the way through. Leave these stitches on the needle. **(a)**

Next, insert the yarn back through the first stitch on the needle as if to knit, and gently pull it all the way through, dropping that stitch off the needle. **(b)**

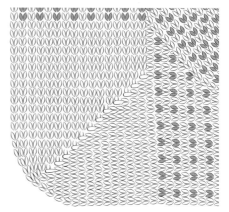

short-row heel with mini gusset

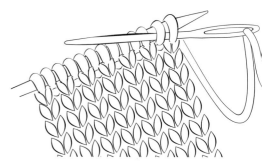

(a) sewn

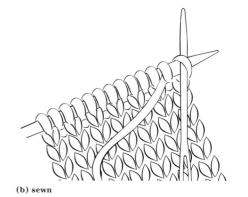

(b) sewn

(c) sewn

Repeat these two steps until you have sewn through all of the stitches. Weave the end of the yarn tail invisibly on the inside of the sock, and trim the end. **(c)**

Note To make the point between the beginning and the end of the cast-off less discernible, after you run the yarn back through the first stitch, move it from the left to the right needle so that it will become the last stitch to be cast off.

russian bind-off The Russian bind-off is another great favorite of mine because it, too, is quick and easy. It has the advantage of being executed without any tools other than your knitting needles. In some instructions for the Russian bind-off, you are told to work the bind-off in purl all the way around or in knit all the way around. When I am doing a ribbed cuff on a sock, I do the bind-off in ribbing, so I knit the knits and purl the purls. When it comes to working the 2 stitches together, I work it knit or purl, depending on what the second stitch of the two is, working the decrease as "knit 2 together through back loops" or "purl 2 together."

In the instructions here, I'm using the word *work* to mean either knit or purl, depending on which stitch presents itself next.

Work 2 and slip these 2 stitches back to the left-hand needle, work 2 together. **(a)**

Now, work 1, and slip the 2 stitches on the right-hand needle back to the left-hand needle, work 2 together. **(b)**

Repeat the second step until you have 1 stitch remaining. Cut the yarn and fasten it off. **(c)**

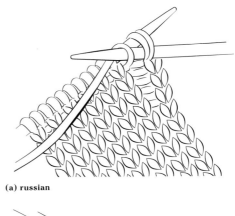

(a) russian

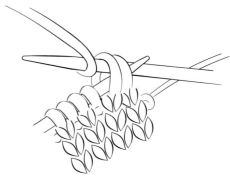

(b) russian

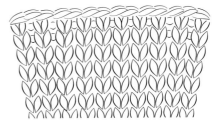

(c) russian

Abbreviations

k—knit

k2tog—knit two together

kf&b—Knit in the front and the back of one stitch to make two stitches.

m1—make one

p—purl

p2tog—purl two together

pf&b—Purl in the front and the back of one stitch to make two stitches.

psso—pass slipped stitch over

sl—slip

ssk—Slip one stitch; then slip the next. Insert the left needle into the front loops of the slipped stitches, and knit them together from this position (through the back loops).

tbl—through back loops

w&t—Wrap and turn. Bring the yarn to the front of the work between needles, slip the next stitch to the right-hand needle, bring the yarn around this stitch to the back of the work, slip the stitch back to the left-hand needle, turn the work to begin working back in the other direction.

yo—yarn over

....

Standard Yarn Weight System

Categories of yarn, gauge ranges, and recommended needle and hook sizes

CYCA	1 SUPER FINE	2 FINE	3 LIGHT	4 MEDIUM	5 BULKY
Yarn Weight	Lace, Fingering, Sock	Sport	DK, Light Worsted	Worsted, Aran	Chunky
Avg. Knitted Gauge over 4" (10cm)	27–32 sts	23–26 sts	21–24 sts	16–20 sts	12–15 sts
Recommended Needle in US Size Range	1–3	3–5	5–7	7–9	9–11
Recommended Needle in Metric Size Range	2.25–3.25mm	3.25–3.75mm	3.75–4.5mm	4.5–5.5mm	5.5–8mm

....

Resources

All of the projects in this book call for materials that are readily available either at local yarn stores or online. The following list of suppliers will help you find all the materials you need to complete the projects in the book. If you have trouble finding a product, consult the websites listed to locate a distributor near you.

Artyarns
www.artyarns.com
914-428-0333

Blue Moon Fiber Arts
www.bluemoonfiberarts.com
503-922-3431

Cherry Tree Hill
www.cherryyarn.com
802-525-3311

Claudia Hand Painted Yarns
www.claudiaco.com
540-433-1140

Dream in Color
www.dreamincoloryarn.com

Fleece Artist
www.fleeceartist.com

Knit One, Crochet Too
www.knitonecrochettoo.com
207-892-9625

Lorna's Laces
www.lornaslaces.net
773-935-3803

Louet
www.louet.com
800-897-6444

Shibui Knits
www.shibuiknits.com
503-595-5898

Acknowledgments

First and foremost I'd like to thank Potter Craft, my publisher. Potter Craft has the reputation for creating stunning, high-quality books, and I am delighted to see my work presented so beautifully.

Thanks also to my editor Rebecca Behan, who has time and time again impressed me with her clarity of thought, attention to detail, and commitment to quality. Rebecca made working through the often tedious but necessary revisions and rewrites almost a pleasure!

I had a mighty band of knitters test these patterns and knit the samples for photography. The WendyKnits knitting brigade consisted of Aimee M. Abernathy, Timmie Ballard, Frances Clement, Erika Connell, Alice Coppa, Brigitte Depocas, Marti Dolezal, Janice Fischer, Sarah Oldenburg Garcia, Dominique Hallett, Sharon Hart, Lindsey-Brooke Hessa, Hariamrit Khalsa, Opal Kiehm, Johanne Ländin, Laura Linneman, Roseann Mauroni, Isobel Thomas, and Ada van Iwaarden.

Thank you one and all!

I owe a special thank-you to Aimee M. Abernathy not only for her willingness and ability to take on extra knitting at the last minute and knock out perfect socks at blazing speed, but for her commitment to quality, her sense of humor, and her concern for my sanity. Thank you, Aimee. I'm proud to call you my friend.

Thank you to Judy Becker for granting me permission to document her fabulous Judy's Magic Cast-On technique in this book.

Thank you to Ian Ories for taking the photographs used to create the illustrations of the techniques demonstrated in this book. This is a tedious chore at best, and Ian has perfected the process, making the photo sessions as painless as possible.

Thank you to Sheri Berger at The Loopy Ewe, who understands exactly how serious it is when I telephone her and whimper "sock yarn emergency!" Not only does she drop everything to express ship sock yarn to me, but she includes chocolate in the package.

And, as in the past, I have depended on my dear friend and knitter extraordinaire Lindsey-Brooke Hessa to take on the duties of technical editor. And as she always has, she rose to the challenge and did a stellar job of proofing, critiquing, and checking my patterns. I always know my work is in good hands when I turn it over to L-B. A technical editor who is so familiar with your work that she knows exactly where to look for your screw-ups and is a good enough friend to be completely honest with you without fear of offending is a rare and wonderful thing. Thank you again, L-B! I couldn't have done it without you.

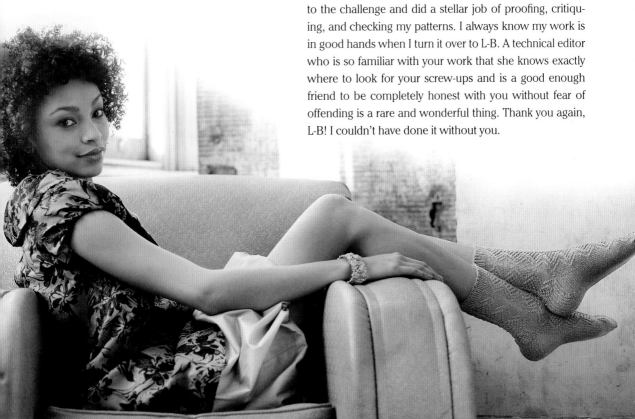

Index

Copyright © 2010 by Wendy D. Johnson

All rights reserved.

Published in the United States by Potter Craft, an imprint of the Crown Publishing Group, a division of Random House, Inc., New York.
www.crownpublishing.com
www.pottercraft.com

POTTER CRAFT and colophon is a registered trademark of Random House, Inc.

Library of Congress Cataloging-in-Publication Data
Johnson, Wendy D.
  Toe-up socks for every body : adventurous lace, cables, and colorwork from Wendy Knits / Wendy D. Johnson. -- 1st ed.
    p. cm.
  Includes index.
  ISBN 978-0-307-46385-2

1. Knitting--Patterns. 2. Socks. I. Title.
TT825.J6485 2009
746.43'2041--dc22

2009029658

Printed in China

Design by La Tricia Watford
Photography by Alexandra Grablewski
Illustrations by Kara Gott Warner

10 9 8 7 6 5 4 3 2 1

First Edition

The author and publisher would like to thank the Craft Yarn Council of America for providing the yarn weight standards and accompanying icons used in this book. For more information, please visit www.YarnStandards.com.